Human Intelligences

ABOUT THE AUTHOR

PANNEER SELVAM is born in Salem - Valappady of Tamil Nadu. He started his career as school teacher in New Delhi in the year 1991. He joins as lecturer in DIET, perundurai of Erode in 2000. Bharathiyar University were gave the Philosophy in Doctorates in Language and Education. He is the seventh diploma holder from National University of Educational Planning and Administration (NUEPA), New Delhi in 2002. In 2005, the Tamil Nadu government was given the 'Excellence Award' for his unrivalled teaching activities and some organization also. He has published more than hundreds of Research Papers and books in the field of Education. At present he is working in the department of Education, Bharathidasan University, Tamil Nadu.

ABOUT THE BOOK

As mentioned in Webster's Dictionary intelligence includes the ability to understand, to apply knowledge, to use reason skillfully, and to manipulate one's environment. The view that intelligence comprises many different abilities is supported by current trends in neurology and cognitive psychology. Among researchers who have identified various types of intelligence, Howard Gardner's (1993) pioneering work at Harvard on multiple intelligences has helped people understand that intelligence is multifaceted. He defines intelligence as "a computational capacity-a capacity to process a certain kind of information-that originates in human biology and human psychology.

The core operations which comprise musical intelligence include the capacities for musical composition, performance, and appreciation, accompanied by skills in the recognition of musical pitch, tone, and rhythm. Most of these elements require that an individual is capable of hearing, yet this is not always the case. In fact, deaf individuals are typically capable of recognizing rhythmic aspects of music in movement and motion.

❐

Human Intelligences

Dr. S.K. Panneer Selvam
Assistant Professor, Department of Education
Bharathidasan University, T.N.,India

AMIGA PRESS INC.

AMIGA PRESS INC.
H.O:- 28-A, Indra Park, St.No-9
Near-Chander Nagar, Krishna Nagar
Delhi: - 110051 (India)
Tel: - 011-22504028, +91-98736-57000
Email: - amigapress@gmail.com
info@amigapress.co.in
amigaeditorial@gmail.com
amigapub@gmail.com

Website: - www.amigapress.co.in

This edition is published by Amiga Press Inc.

ISBN: 978-93-84533-67-0

First Published 2020

Printed and bound in India by Replika Press Pvt. Ltd.

Contents

1. **The Oretical Frame work** 1

Types of intelligence' Concept of existential thinking; How to experience sq; Transcendence; Sanctification; Spirituality as problem solving skill; Spirituality as ethical and virtuous behaviour; Full spectrum of intelligence; Components of spiritual intelligence; Elements of spiritual intelligence; The four dimensions of spiritual intelligence; Personal meaning production; Transcendental awareness; Conscious state expansion; Recommendations to improve sq; Twelve principles of sq; Concept of goal orientation; Mastery vs performance goals; Which is best? Mastery or performance goals; Multiple-goals dilemma; Recent conceptualizations; Goal orientation in communications; Learning-approach and learning-avoidance; Prove performance goal orientation; Avoid performance; Need for achievements; Academic outcomes; Organizational outcomes; Temperament; Thurstone temperament schedule (tts); The four temperament types; Delimitation of the study; Conclusion.

2. **Review of Literature** 30

Significance of the study; Studies related to spiritual intelligence; Studies related to goal orientation; Studies related to temperament; Conclusion.

3. **Research Design and Methods of Investigation** 51

According to thyer, Need for research design; Design of the study; Hypotheses of the study; Hypothesis of the study; Tools and techniques used; Spiritual intelligence scale; Scoring procedures of spiritual intelligence; Goal orientation scale; Administration; Temperament inventory scale; Scoring procedure used for measure the temperament of higher secondary school students; Sample of the study; Distribution of the sampleArithmetic mean; Formula to find coefficient of correlation; Conclusion.

4. **Analysis and Interpretation of Data** **61**
Categorization of the sample based on the variables of the study; Influence of medium of instructions on spiritual intelligence and its dimensions; Influence of type of management on spiritual intelligence and its; dimensions; Inference; Influence of type of family on spiritual intelligence and its dimensions; Influence of family monthly income on spiritual intelligence and its dimensions; Influence of gender on goal orientation; Influence of type of management on goal orientation; Inference; Influence of type of family on goal orientation; Influence of family monthly income on goal orientation; Influence of type of managementt on temperamentt anditsdimension;Inference;Influenceoftypeofmanagementtontemperamentt and its dimension; Conclusion.

5. **Summary, Finding, Discussion, Implications, Suggestions and Conclusion** **86**
Statement of the problem; Objectives of the study; Hypotheses of the study Sample of the study; Tools and techniques used; Collection of data; Analysis of data; Major findings of spiritual intelligence in relation to goal orientation and temperament; Discussions on spiritual intelligence; Discussions on goal orientation; Discussions on temperament; Educational implications of the study on spiritual intelligencein relation to goal-orientation and temperament; Conclusion.

6. **The Problem and its Perspectives** **97**
Meaning of social intelligence; Definition of social intelligence; Needs of social intelligence; Development of social intelligence; Factors of social intelligence; Meaning of self-esteem; Definitions on self-esteem; Psychological background of self-esteem; Development of self-esteem; Phases of self-esteem; Types of self-esteem; Self-esteem in adolescents; Statement of the problem; Operational definitions; Objectives of the study; Need for the study; Delimitations of the study; Conclusion.

7. **Review of Related Literature** **106**
Role of related literature in a research project; Studies related to social intelligence; Studies in india; Studies related to self-esteem; Studies in india; Conclusion.

8. Research Design and Methodology **117**
Variables selected; Hypotheses of the study; Method of study; Tools used; Social intelligence scale; Self-esteem scale; Sample distribution; Pilot study; Reliability and validity of the tools; Social intelligence; Self-esteem Main study; Statistical techniques used; Conclusion.

9. Analysis and Interpretation of the Data **127**
Descriptive analysis ; Influence of gender on social intelligence; Influence of type of management onsocial intelligence; Influence of type of father's educational qualification on social intelligence; Inference;Influence of mother's educational qualification on social intelligence; Inference; Influence of birth orderonsocial intelligence; Influenceof family monthly incomeonsocial intelligence; Inference; Conclusion.

10. Summary Findings Conclusion **139**
Statement of the problem; Operational definitions; Objectives of the study Hypotheses of the study; Tools used; Major findings; Educational implications; Delimitations of the study; Suggestions for furthuer research; Conclusion.

11. The Problem and its Perspectives **146**
The concept of emotional competence; Meaning of emotional competence; The nature of emotions; Effects of emotion; Personal competence; Social competence; Personal competence; Self-regulation; Self-motivation; Social competence; Social skills; Criteria for assessing emotional competency; Importance of leadership; Objectives of the study; Conclusion.

12. Review of Related Literature **157**
Studies related to emotional competence; Studies related to leaderspip preference; Conclusion.

13. Design and Method of Investigation **169**
Hypotheses of the study; Tools and techniques used; Leadership preference inventory; Pilot study; Establishing reliability and validity; Main study Statistical techniques used; Conclusion.

14. Analysis and Interpretation of Data **176**
Classification of the sample based on the; variables of the study; Emotional competence; Influence of gender on emotional competence; Inference; Influence of birth order on emotional competency; Influence of type of family on emotional competence; Influence of birth order on leadership preference; Inference; Influence of type of family on leadership preference;Conclusion.

15. Summary, Findings and Conclusion **185**
Statement of the problem; Objectives of the study; Hypotheses of the study; Sample of the study; Tools and techniques used; Major findings; Educational implications; Suggestions for further research; Conclusion.

Bibliography **189**

❐

1

The Oretical Frame Work

In 1905 Alfred Binet and Theodore Simon developed the first modern intelligence test. Since then the word intelligence was mostly associated with intellect and used to describe the capacities of our rational mind to understand, reason, create ideas, plan, solve problems, learn or use language. Intelligence is sometimes defined as the ability to manage cognitive complexity. As mentioned in Webster's Dictionary intelligence includes the ability to understand, to apply knowledge, to use reason skillfully, and to manipulate one's environment. The view that intelligence comprises many different abilities is supported by current trends in neurology and cognitive psychology. Among researchers who have identified various types of intelligence, Howard Gardner's (1993) pioneering work at Harvard on multiple intelligences has helped people understand that intelligence is multifaceted. He defines intelligence as "a computational capacity-a capacity to process a certain kind of information-that originates in human biology and human psychology. Intelligence entails the ability to solve problems or fashion products that are of consequence in a particular cultural setting or community" (Gardner, 1993: 6). Gardner's research indicates that different kinds of intelligence develop relatively independently of each other, and proficiency in one area does not imply proficiency in another. For example, linguistic skill with words can be differentiated from logical mathematical skill with numbers and from the spatial intelligence that perceives spatial relationships. Excellence in one area does not necessarily tell us anything about abilities in another. In addition, Gardner (1993) discussed kinesthetic intelligence that enables a person to use the body in highly differentiated and skilled ways, such as dance or athletics; musical intelligence necessary for all different kinds of musical aptitude; intrapersonal intelligence that implies awareness of one's own thoughts and feelings; and interpersonal intelligence that enables us to relate to others empathically. He did not discuss spiritual intelligence as a separate line of development.

THE HIERARCHY OF FOUR HUMAN INTELLIGENCES

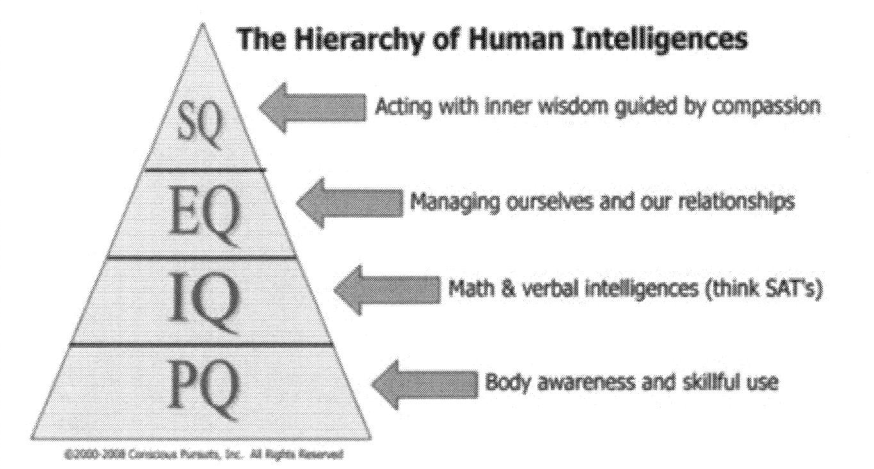

Fig. 1.1: The Hierarchy of Four Human Intelligences

IMAGE OF SPIRITUAL INTELLIGENCE

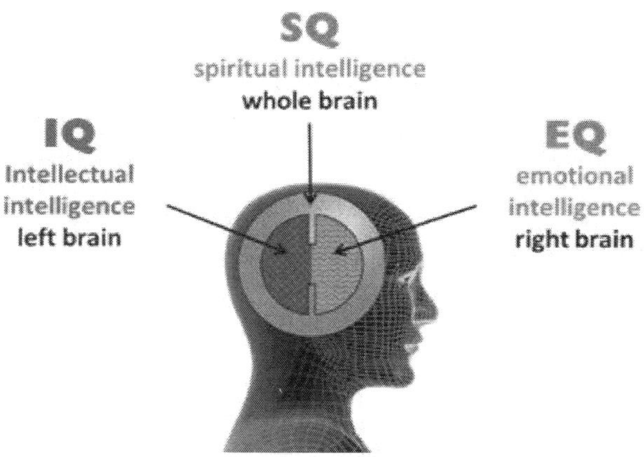

Fig. 1.2: Spiritual Intelligence: Spiritual intelligence has access to advanced capabilities from a higher dimension of intelligence.

Benefits of SQ

- Feels greater fulfilment
- Finds deeper meaning and purpose
- Turns negative into positive thoughts & emctions
- Employs his full resources and be his best in any situation
- Wisdom, ompassion
- Integrity • Joy • Love • Creativity • Peace
- Helps others and improves society by using a higher dimension of his intelligence

TYPES OF INTELLIGENCE

Multiple Intelligences

Gardner (1983) makes an important note about the difference between "know-how" (procedural knowledge of how to execute a task) and "know-that" (propositional knowledge about the procedures involved). His multiple intelligences should be viewed as sets of procedural knowledge. Finally, he warns that the intelligences in his theory are nothing more than "useful fictions" (Gardner, 1983: 70) for discussing sets of interrelated mental abilities. They exist only as scientific constructs and should not be thought of as physical entities, as this has yet to be verified (Gardner, 1983).

This inquiry into spiritual intelligence suggests that it is one of several types of intelligence and that it can be developed relatively independently. Spiritual intelligence calls for multiple ways of knowing and for the integration of the inner life of mind and spirit with the outer life of work in the world. It can be cultivated through questing, inquiry and practice. Spiritual experiences may also contribute to its development, depending on the context and means of integration. Spiritual maturity is expressed through wisdom and compassionate action in the world. Spiritual intelligence is necessary for discernment in making spiritual choices that contribute to psychological well-being and overall healthy spiritual development.

Linguistic Intelligence

The core abilities which compose linguistic intelligence include: a sensitivity to the meaning of words (i.e., semantics); a sensitivity to the order and arrangement of letters and words (e.g. phonology, spelling, grammar, syntax); a sensitivity to the sounds of words (e.g., rhythms and inflections); and a sensitivity to the many functions of language (i.e., pragmatics). Other important uses noted by Gardner (1983) include the ability to use language to convince others of a desired course of action, the capacity to use mnemonics to facilitate memorization of information, and the capacity for meta- linguistics. He further, adds that pragmatics include input from some of the other intelligences, such as interpersonal intelligence, and the case for an autonomous linguistic intelligence is most convincing when looking at phonological and syntactic abilities.

Logical-Mathematical Intelligence

Logical-mathematical intelligence consists of the capacity to analyze problems logically, carry out mathematical operations, and investigate issues scientifically. It includes the ability to detect patterns, reason deductively, and think logically, and is most often associated with scientific and mathematical ways of thinking. Gardner (1983) relies heavily on Piaget's (1963) stage theory of intellectual competence for both descriptions of these abilities as well as support for the developmental history of logical-mathematical intelligence. He reviews Piaget's theory in detail and defines his formal operations stage as the expert end-state for this ability set (Gardner, 1983).

Spatial Intelligence

The core abilities of spatial intelligence include the capacity to perceive the world accurately, the capacity to perform transformations and modifications upon one's initial perceptions and the ability to recreate aspects of one's visual experience (even in the absence of the stimuli in question). While these abilities all appear to include some visual perception, Gardner (1983) suggests that this is not so, as there are documented cases of blind individuals who still demonstrate high spatial abilities using tactile senses. All abilities are useful in orienting oneself in a new environment, comparing or contrasting two forms, or being attentive to balance and composition, as in the case of artwork (Gardner,1983: 170-204).

Musical INtelligence

The core operations which comprise musical intelligence include the capacities for musical composition, performance, and appreciation, accompanied by skills in the recognition of musical pitch, tone, and rhythm. Most of these elements require that an individual is capable of hearing, yet this is not always the case. In fact, deaf individuals are typically capable of recognizing rhythmic aspects of music in movement and motion. In spite of some subjective problems in the perception of music, research has shown that nearly all people are able to agree upon their perception of good music (Gardner,1983: 99-127).

Bodily-Kinesthetic Intelligence

Gardner (1983) only discusses two core operations involved in bodily-kinesthetic intelligence: the capacity to control one's bodily motions and the capacity to handle objects skillfully. Included in these capacities are the abilities to judge timing, force, extent of movements, and to subsequently make the appropriate physical adjustments. Although Western culture tends to draw a sharp distinction between the mental and the physical, he suggests that this is not the case in most cultures.

Intrapersonal Intelligence

According to Gardner (1983), the core capacity of intrapersonal intelligence is the ability to access one's own feelings and affects. This is accompanied by the capacity to discriminate among these feelings, to label them, and to draw upon them in order to guide behaviour. Basic capacities, therefore, include the ability to distinguish pleasure from pain and to become more or less involved in a situation. Higher abilities include detecting, symbolizing, and distinguishing between more complex sets of emotions.

Interpersonal Intelligence

Interpersonal intelligence is essentially the external application of intrapersonal abilities. Included is the capacity to notice and make distinctions among other individuals, particularly their emotions and mood states, temperaments, motivations, and intentions. At a more extreme end, it also includes the capacity to influence others and convince them to behave according to one's desires. Gardner's (1983) interpersonal intelligence is largely comparable to Thorndike's (1920) social intelligence.

Naturalist Intelligence

After much deliberation, Gardner (1993) eventually accepted an eighth intelligence on his list of multiple intelligences. Naturalist intelligence enables human beings to recognize, categorize, and draw upon features of the environment, whether these features be plants, animals, mountains, or cloud formations. These abilities are not restricted to vision alone, but can be based on any of the senses, including audition, as in the case of classifying bird calls. He suggests that in developed countries, naturalist abilities have simply taken a unique form; that our consumer culture is based on the naturalist intelligence, being used each time we shop for groceries or buy one car rather than another.

Moral INtelligence

Gardner (1997, 1999) has also considered a moral intelligence as a potential candidate in his model. He doubts, however, the possibility of delineating a moral domain from other domains and establishing moral intelligence as an autonomous construct. According to him, the moral domain "is a concern with those rules, behaviours and attitudes that govern the sanctity of life - in particular, the sanctity of human life and, in many cases, the sanctity of any other living creature and the world they inhabit" (Gardner, 1999: 70). He further contends that morality is more an issue of personality and character than it is an issue of intelligence, therefore denying its place in multiple intelligence theory (Gardner, 1999).

Existential Intelligence

Existential intelligence can be defined as the ability to be sensitive to, or have the capacity for, conceptualizing or tackling deeper or larger questions about human existence, such as the meaning of life, why are we born, why do we die, what is consciousness, or how did we get here.

Existential intelligence can be defined as the ability to be sensitive to, or have the capacity for, conceptualizing or tackling deeper or larger questions about human existence, such as the meaning of life, why are we born, why do we die, what is consciousness, or how did we get here. Sep. 455

Existential Intelligence Definition

Existential intelligence is one of Howard Gardner's Nine Multiple Intelligences. It involves an individual's ability to use collective values and intuition to understand others and the world around them. Individuals who excel in this intelligence typically are able to see the big picture. Philosophers, theologians, and life coaches are among those that Howard Gardner sees as having high existential intelligence.

"The possibility of "existential" intelligence has been alluded to by Gardner in several of his works. He has stated that existential intelligence might be manifest in someone who is concerned with fundamental questions about existence, or who questions the intricacies of existence."

Existential intelligence is defined as the ability to be sensitive to, or have the capacity for, conceptualizing or tackling deeper or larger questions about human existence, such as the meaning of life, why are we born, why do we die, what is consciousness, or how did we get here.

CONCEPT OF EXISTENTIAL THINKING

Existential intelligence is an individual's capacity or ability to understand and contemplate philosophical topics relating to mankind's existence. According to the theory of existential intelligence, some individuals have an easier time conceptualizing deep philosophical questions, such as the origin of mankind, what constitutes consciousness, and man's purpose on earth. Those individuals with a strong tendency toward existential intelligence are, according to some experts, more inclined to ask questions regarding these ultimate realities, including the meaning of life.

In terms of the origin of existential intelligence, the concept is tied to philosophical theories as well as the theory of multiple intelligences. Regarding the concept's definition, this type of intelligence draws on many of the same questions and topics associated with existentialism, a method of philosophical inquiry popularized in the 1940s and 1950s. Existentialism proposes that human existence cannot be defined by spiritual or scientific categories currently in existence, but rather requires a deeper understanding. Using existentialism as a basis of understanding, the concept of existential intelligence is then associated with Gardner's theory of multiple intelligences.

Howard Gardner of Harvard University first presented the idea of multiple intelligences in the early 1980s. Education and psychology experts had sought a better understanding of the natural way children think and learn, so Gardner developed a theory to help identify the strongest tendencies in school age children. Initially, Gardner presented the concept of seven intelligences, including logical or mathematical, spatial, musical, and others. The theory of multiple intelligences was designed to explain different types of learning modalities and thus allow educators to develop learning plans to work with the strengths of each child. After introducing his theory of multiple intelligences, Gardner and other education and psychology experts continued researching the concept. Several professionals, including Gardner, later proposed additional types of intelligence. Although Gardner neither publicly nor officially included existential intelligence in his revised theory, he and other professionals discussed its existence. While remaining unofficial in terms of including existential intelligence in his theory, Gardner proposed a definition for the concept if it were to be included with his other intelligences.

Since the theory of multiple intelligences centers on education and early childhood psychology, some experts argue the validity of including existential intelligence with Gardner's other intelligences. Deep philosophical questions regarding mankind's existence often stir intense, passionate debate, a prospect some experts argue has no place in childhood education. Avoiding such debates is the primary reason most experts decline to add existential intelligence to the greater theory of multiple intelligences. Consideration of an existential intelligence stemmed from earlier claims of a spiritual intelligence. Reportedly, Gardner (1993) devoted a year of study to the investigation of this topic, coming to the conclusion that a spiritual intelligence did not meet his eight criteria. In spite of this, one facet of spirituality proved a promising candidate for Gardner (1993): existential intelligence. He describes this as "the intelligence of big questions" (Gardner, 1993: 20), based on the human tendency to contemplate the most fundamental questions of life. Gardner (1993) contends that an existential intelligence scores reasonably well on his eight criteria, noting that such issues arise in every culture and that children often raise these questions at an early age. Individuals with exceptional existential abilities can be noted throughout history, such as religious leaders and philosophers. Nevertheless, he hesitates to include existential intelligence in his list, maintaining that evidence is lacking as to possible brain localization. He is often quoted as stating that until such evidence is found, he will continue speaking of "eight and a half intelligences" (Gardner, 1993: Daniel Goleman's(1995) research on emotional intelligence, based primarily on intrapersonal and interpersonal intelligence, indicates that success in many areas of life depends on emotional skills as much as on cognitive capacities. Emotional intelligence includes self-awareness and self-control, as well as the ability to get along well with others. Getting along with others implies an ability to listen, to communicate, to accept feedback, and to empathize with different points of view. According to Goleman and others, different kinds of intelligence are associated with different areas of the brain. Although little research has been done to isolate areas of the brain associated with spirituality, numerous studies in meditation research indicate that significant physiological changes result from even limited practice (Murphy & Donovan, 1999; Shapiro & Walsh, 1984; Walsh & Vaughan, 1993). Studies that measure the effects of intensive, long-term practice point to significant psychological benefits in addition to deepening emotional and spiritual sensitivity (Vaughan, 2002).

Spiritual Intelligence

Even though humanity has reached the age of wisdom, many cultures of today are still characterized as "left-brained", material or "spiritually stunted." Due to these problems in the fabric of daily life, quite a number of people are making an effort to find ways to re-connect with their essence, attain a higher meaning in life, manage uncertainties successfully with inner poise, and in short to undergo an "inner change." Fortunately this inner change has begun for many. Spiritual intelligence (SQ) took the leading role in this great transformation process, since SQ necessitates our perception, provides the key to changing feeling, understanding and behavior. In other words SQ serves as an inner compass that facilitates the integration of subjective insights and illuminations with ways of being and acting in the world (Dincer, 2007). A higher level of intelligence power distinguishes human beings from other animals on this planet. It has been the favourite subject of research for psychologists. In the20th century, they created IQ tests to define and measure intelligence power of an individual. But, it proved inadequate for measuring the wide spectrum of intelligence.

Functions of Spiritual Intelligence

SQ regulates IQ and EQ with wisdom, compassion, and integrity. SQ thus provides access to advanced human capabilities. Spiritual intelligence therefore represents the most powerful resource for personal and professional success and fulfillment. SQ results in cooperation and tolerance between people, not only at the interpersonal level, but also between different groups in society, and between different cultures and nations. When SQ sets the social norms across entire communities, transformation follows at the level of social institutions and international relations, as governments are repurposed and corporations are reformed according to spiritually intelligent principles. Widespread practice of spiritual intelligence is therefore necessary and sufficient for individual and collective transformation.

HOW TO EXPERIENCE SQ

At times we all experience spiritual intelligence spontaneously. But spontaneous moments of SQ are rare, and they usually occur at random. Therefore it's important to know how to experience SQ intentionally. When you can engage your spiritual intelligence voluntarily, in any circumstances, you convert your SQ from a random fleeting experience into your most valuable, powerful, and useful personal resource.

Mystical experiences and mysticism are everyday experiences of human beings. Mysticism is not limited to monastics, nor to peoples enclosed in an ashram, a cave in the desert or some monastery atop a mountain. Divinity is always divinity in ordinary, for all life is imbued with divinity. Humankind, in their multiform and variegated quests for divinity, have not the right to limit divinity and where divine encounters occur; humankind is limited, however, by their own perception and understanding. This aside, nothing controls, prohibits, decides nor limits when and where Divinity elects to make itself manifest or encountered.

Mystical experiences occur when one leaves behind the sense of bodily awareness and encounters divinity as it reveals itself within and without. One may see divinity all around. One may perceive divine manifestations, spiritual dreams, miracles and divine interventions in your life or the life of another are evidence of mystical experiences. These can also be encountered via - but not limited to - meditation, chanting of prayers, mantras, use of rosary beads, japamala or other kinds of prayer wheels or sacred ‹counters›.

TRANSCENDENCE

Transcendence means going beyond, moving past the inward focus of the self to encounter other selves, and the Self in the other. It does not imply refuting nor rejecting any foundation, or being «other than»; rather, it means being larger than any container of belief. Hence, transcendence as a part of Spiritual Intelligence means encounter and experience beyond the normal religious container.

Transcendence is selfless service of the other; feeding and clothing the poor, visiting the elderly in nursing homes, visiting the sick in hospital and day care or after care, visiting the imprisoned. It is engagement in charitable works for the benefit of society at large. It is participation in workshops on spiritual topics and going on spiritual retreats. It is prayer and meditation in common, and participating in group prayers and prayers in the public domain.

Interfaith activity, multi-faith events and inter-religious dialogue are vital elements of transcendence. In dialogue and encounter with people of other faith or spiritual traditions, the experience of the participant is enlarged to witness the experience of the person or faith group being encountered; it is also, almost always, an encounter with one's own self as the task of describing personal spirituality to others is always self-enlarging, and always, an experience of transcendence. One recognizes the Divine in the encounter and dialogue with those of other spiritualities.

SANCTIFICATION

Sanctify, Latin: sanctify-care to make holy or treat as holy, to sanctify, consecrate, dedicate. The Latin Sanctus means: to sanctify, to make holy, hallow, or keep holy. So we understand that sanctification means to render holy, impart sanctity to (a thing, quality, action or condition); to impart real or apparent sacredness to; to entitle to reverence or respect; to give a colour of morality or innocence to; to justify, sanction.

Acts of sanctification include morning and evening devotions, prayers, mediations, chanting, counting of rosary beads or japa or use of prayer wheels; prayers before meals; daily prayers for peace in the world; daily affirmations of love and light towards one, or many, in one's world, or indeed, one's worldwide home, Mother Earth. Sanctification is evoked by daily sacred reading, self-dedication to the Divine, and participation in sacred study groups. Sanctification sees all as acts of the Divine; there are no actions or accidents which are unplanned; all is planned by the Divine.

Sanctification has an element of surrender to the Divine. One need not surrender one's intellect nor uncritically follow the guidelines of religious leaders. There is no chance of being misled or mistaken. At every step, one has to rely on one's own intellect and experience, as tested by one. Spirituality is experience, one's own, personal experience.

SPIRITUALITY AS PROBLEM SOLVING SKILL

The elements of mystical experiences, transcendence and sanctification build what you might call your spiritual credit. When you make withdrawals at a bank the teller (or the automatic transaction machine - ATM) makes reference to your credit and processes the transaction thereby. When problems and challenges confront a person with spiritual resources, then one may draw on these resources (spiritual credits) for the solution, for strength, for energy, for perseverance and endurance. Personal experience generates spiritual credit against which one may make withdrawals. Thus, spirituality becomes a resource for handling the everyday problems of living, for handling challenges, stress, trauma, accidents, disappointments, and the foundation to choose how one may act when encountering these or any other situations. The foundation of mind-management is present when such a spiritual credit is established within. There is a clear distinction between the mind and the consciousness which is established by this «spiritual credit» as we call it.

SPIRITUALITY AS ETHICAL AND VIRTUOUS BEHAVIOUR

Spirituality is acting with common sense and spiritual sense. All action reveals a person's choices and their values. Choices are always based on what is good for the person, what they value. Hasty action and thoughtless action produces hasty results and thoughtless results that which may fail to satisfy the Higher Self within. Cultivation of Self-directed behaviour produces ethical and virtuous behaviour. Morality does not merely mean the observance of certain rules in the work-a-day world. Morality means adherence to the straight and sacred path of spiritual effort. Morality is the blossoming of good conduct. There are no universal and absolute norms of morality. Ethical relativity is an inescapable social phenomenon. Morality depends on the time, the place, and the spirit of the age.

The habit of spirituality developing ethical and virtuous behaviour produces integrity. Integrity is unity of thoughts, words and actions, what is called good character or human excellence.

These character traits are elicited by self-monitoring, self-regulation and self-review or self-audit. The cultivation of these skills and habits forms the strings of connections between conscious, conscience and consciousness; wherein one will always be acting in accord with the Higher Self. This is spirituality in action.

Why "Q"?

Why is "SQ" the abbreviation for spiritual intelligence rather than "SI"? The letter "Q" stands for "quotient" which means amount or score. Thus IQ means your intellectual intelligence quotient, or your IQ score. Similarly, EQ means your emotional intelligence quotient, and SQ means your spiritual intelligence quotient. Usually the term "SQ" is read simply as "spiritual intelligence", leaving the word "quotient" unspoken.

FULL SPECTRUM OF INTELLIGENCE

3Q Training SQ combined with IQ and EQ represent the three Qs, which together activate the whole brain, unlike IQ or EQ on their own, which are part-brain functions. By training the whole brain, 3Q Training unlocks advanced capabilities, which increase personal fulfilment and result.

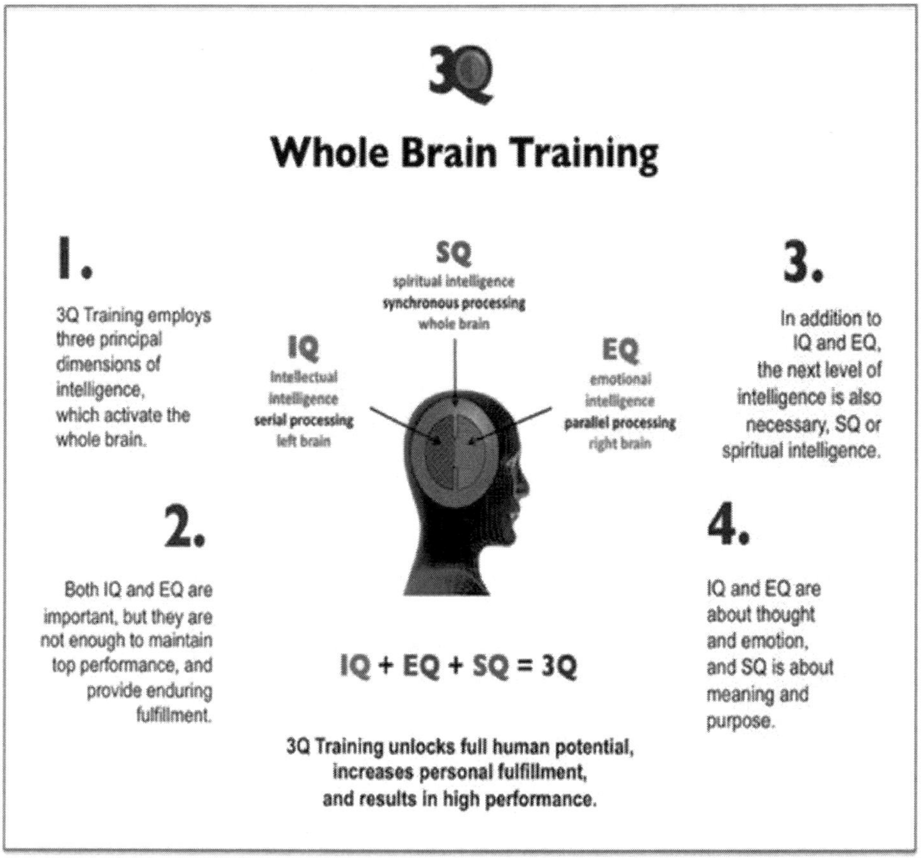

Fig. 1.3: Whole Brain Training

SQ AND THE BRAIN

Neurologically SQ is distinct from IQ and EQ. Opposite hemispheres are the primary locations for IQ and EQ, whereas SQ is associated with hemispheric synchronization and whole-brain activation at particular frequencies. SQ whole-brain frequencies combine part-brain functions, such as IQ and EQ, from both hemispheres, into the integrated field of the whole brain, thus combining mind, self, and world into a meaningful whole. SQ neural frequencies correspond to the same brain state underlying the practice of meditation and the experience of presence. SQ capability is therefore hard-wired in the human brain. Spiritual intelligence is necessary and sufficient for individual and collective transformation.

COMPONENTS OF SPIRITUAL INTELLIGENCE

Self / Self-Awareness

1. Awareness of own worldview
2. Awareness of life purpose (mission)
3. Awareness of values hierarchy
4. Complexity of inner thought
5. Awareness of ego self / higher self

Universal Awareness

1. Awareness of interconnectedness of life
2. Awareness of worldviews of others
3. Breadth of time perception
4. Awareness of limitations / power of human perception
5. Awareness of spiritual laws
6. Experience of transcendent oneness

Self/ Self-Mastery

1. Commitment to spiritual growth
2. Keeping higher self in charge
3. Living your purpose and values
4. Sustaining faith
5. Seeking guidance from spirit

Social Mastery/Spiritual Presence

1. Wise and effective teacher / mentor
2. Wise and effective leader / change agent
3. Makes compassionate and wise decisions
4. A calming, healing presence
5. Being aligned with the ebb and flow of life

ELEMENTS OF SPIRITUAL INTELLIGENCE

Gardner and Evans investigated spiritual intelligence and arrived at five core components:

- Mystical experiences
- Transcendence
- Sanctification
- As a resource to solve problems
- Ethical and virtuous behavior

Traits of Those Who Have High Existential Intelligence:

- Sees the big picture
- Interested in questions about life, death, and beyond
- Able to look beyond the senses to explain phenomena
- Likes to Be Outside
- Strong interest in society and those around them

THE FOUR DIMENSIONS OF SPIRITUAL INTELLIGENCE

Critical Existential Thinking

The capacity to critically contemplate the nature of existence, reality, the universe, space, time, and other existential/metaphysical issues and also the capacity to contemplate non-existential issues in relation to one's existence (i.e., from an existential perspective).Chance (1986) defined critical thinking as "the ability to analyze facts, generate and organize ideas, defend opinions, make comparisons, draw inferences, evaluate arguments and solve problems" (Chance, 1986: 6).

Concept of Critical Existential Thinking

Existential intelligence is an individual's capacity or ability to understand and contemplate philosophical topics relating to mankind's existence. According to the theory of existential intelligence, some individuals have an easier time conceptualizing deep philosophical questions, such as the origin of mankind, what constitutes consciousness, and man's purpose on earth. Those individuals with a strong tendency toward existential intelligence are, according to some experts, more inclined to ask questions regarding these ultimate realities, including the meaning of life.

PERSONAL MEANING PRODUCTION

The ability to derive the personal meaning and purpose from all the physical and mental experiences, including the capacity to create and master a life purpose. While one may be able to derive purpose from daily events and experiences, one may also be able to define a purpose for his/her life. This likely involves more coherent and creative forms of meaning production. The mastering of a purpose refers to one's ability to infer his/her purpose in all events and experiences.

Personal meaning production is defined as the ability to construct personal meaning and purpose in all physical and mental experiences, including the capacity to create and master a life purpose. The construct is explored as a component of spiritual intelligence (i.e., a mental capacity), offering support according to established criteria for intelligence. Evidence of cognitive operations and adaptive applications, including problem-solving and coping, is reviewed in detail. Personal meaning production appears to be highly adaptive in crises of an existential or spiritual nature, as well as problems related to physical and psychological health. Due to the seemingly infinite number of sources of personal meaning, it is argued that deriving meaning from all experiences represents the high end-state of this ability. It is further maintained that this capacity represents a highly viable and necessary component of spiritual intelligence, without which the portrait of human mentation is incomplete.

In an attempt to accurately re-conceptualize the construct, spiritual intelligence is currently defined as a set of adaptive mental capacities which contribute to the awareness, integration, and adaptive application of the nonmaterial and transcendent aspects of one's existence, leading to such outcomes as deep existential reflection, enhancement of meaning, recognition of a transcendent self, and mastery of spiritual states. Four core components are proposed: critical existential thinking, personal meaning production, transcendental awareness, and conscious state expansion. The current paper will focus on the capacity of personal meaning production, which is defined as the ability to construct personal meaning and purpose in all physical and mental experiences, including the capacity to create and master a life purpose.

TRANSCENDENTAL AWARENESS

The capacity to identify transcendent dimensions/patterns of the self (i.e. transpersonal or transcendent self), of others, and of the physical world (e.g. non-materialism) during normal states of consciousness, accompanied by the capacity to identify their relationship to one's self and to the physical.

CONSCIOUS STATE EXPANSION

The ability to enter and exit higher states of consciousness (e.g. pure consciousness, cosmic consciousness, unity, oneness) and other states trance at one's own discretion (as in deep contemplation, meditation, prayer, etc.).

RECOMMENDATIONS TO IMPROVE SQ

Since SQ positively impacts QoL, it is imperative that we live a fulfilling and satisfying life by enhancing SQ because that is the underpinning factor. The brain is wired for SQ but it remains dormant and needs to be activated. It takes effort and time to develop SQ but it is worth the effort realizing its benefits. Some of the methods available are discussed in the succeeding text.

Meditation

Several methods are available for meditation. One may choose that suits him the best. If much time cannot be invested in meditation, duration of 20 minutes is considered to be optimal. Sri SriRavi Shankar asserts that meditation improves and balances physical, mental, emotional and spiritual spheres of a man.

Prayers

For those who believe in God, prayer includes respect, love, pleading and faith. Through a prayer a devotee endows the doer ship of the task to God. Giving the doer ship to God means that we acknowledge that God is helping us and getting the task done. Prayer is an important tool of spiritual practice in the generic spiritual path of devotion. Prayer reduces worry and enhances contemplation.

Tools to Empower

One may choose any tool to enhance his SQ and QoL, for it will lead him to satisfying and purposeful life. Among others, Reiki is a simple and easy - to - learn technique for better life and pleasant experiences.

Observance of Spiritual Values / Qualities

A dual approach may be of enormous benefit for spiritual seekers. One, SQ may be enhanced by the techniques stated above and then manifest the spiritual values in day to day behaviour. Second, consciously, practice the spiritual values / qualities in everyday life and increase the SQ, leading to a positive virtuous spiral.

TWELVE PRINCIPLES OF SQ

1	Self-awareness	Knowing what I believe in, value, and deeply motivates me
2	Vision and Value Led	acting from principles and deep beliefs, and living accordingly
3	Positive use of Adversity	Learning and growing from mistakes, setbacks, and suffering.

4	Holistic	seeing larger patterns, relationships, and connections; having a sense of belonging
5	Compassion	Having the quality of "feeling – with" and deep empathy.
6	Celebration of Diversity	Regarding other people for their differences, not despite them.
7	Field-Independent	Standing against the crowd and having one's own convictions.
8	Ask Fundamental "Why" questions	Needing to understand things and get to the bottom of them.
9	Ability to Reframe	Standing back from a situation/ problem and seeing the bigger picture; seeing problems in a wider context.
10	Spontaneity	Living in and being responsive to the moment.
11	Sense of Vocation	Feeling called upon to serve, to give something back.
12	Humility	Having the sense of being a player in a larger drama, of one's true place in the world.

CONCEPT OF GOAL ORIENTATION

Goal orientation is a "disposition toward developing or demonstrating ability in achievement situations". Previous research has examined goal orientation as a motivationvariable useful for recruitment, climate and culture, performance appraisal, and selection. Studies have also used goal orientation to predict sales performance, goal, learning and adaptive behaviors in training, and leadership. Due to the many theoretical and practical applications of goal orientation, it is important to understand the construct and how it relates to other variables. In this entry, goal orientation will be reviewed in terms of its history, stability, dimensionality, antecedents, its relationship to goal setting and consequences, its relevance to motivation, and future directions for research.

Most of human behavior is directed by goals and needs. Goals range from personal to professional, from being happy to doing well in school, from short-term to long-term and the list could go on and on. Needs can be objective and physical or subjective and psychological. This lesson will distinguish between the constructs of goals and needs. It is also seen that different types of goals as they relate to academics and learning.

The concept of need assumes a slightly different definition. To psychologists, a need is a psychological feature that drives a human or animal toward a goal or behavior. Examples of this definition include a need for achievement, a need for affiliation with others and a need for attention.

Goal orientation theory is a social-cognitive theory of achievement motivation. Goal theory became a particularly important theoretical framework in the study of academic motivation in the late 1980s. Whereas other motivational theories examine students› beliefs about their successes and failures, goal orientation theory examines the reasons why students engage in their academic work.

A core goal is a long-term goal that drives much of what an individual does. These long-term goals help direct behavior toward achievement and success. Let›s meet Jack. Jack is a freshman in college. Jack wants to go to medical school after completing his undergraduate degree. Jack›s core goal is to get accepted into the most prestigious medical school in the country.

Short-term goals, referred to as proximal goals, are more concrete and can be accomplished within a short time period. One can think of proximal goals as a stepping stone toward a longer-range goal. Jack has many proximal goals in order to help him achieve his core goal of getting accepted into a prestigious medical school. He has a GPA goal of 4.0 for his first semester in college, a goal of taking the MCATs within two years and a goal of volunteering 50 hours a semester at the local hospital. All of these goals can be achieved in a short duration of time and will ultimately help Jack achieve his core goal.

MASTERY VS PERFORMANCE GOALS

The work of early goal theorists contrasted two types of goal orientations: mastery, which is a desire to acquire additional knowledge or master new skills, and performance, which is a desire to demonstrate high ability and make a good impression. Recent works of goal theorists have incorporated a second dimension of goal orientations: approach and avoidance.

Mastery-oriented goals are defined in terms of a focus on learning, mastering the task according to self-set standards or self-improvement. It also encompasses developing new skills, improving or developing competence, trying to accomplish something challenging and trying to gain an understanding or insight.

Performance-oriented goals represent a focus on demonstrating competence or ability and how ability will be judged relative to others. For example, trying to surpass normative performance standards, attempting to best others, using casual comparative standards or striving to be the best in a group or even avoiding judgments of low ability or appearing dumb are examples of performance-oriented goals.

Approach-oriented goals are goals in which individuals are positively motivated to look good and receive favorable judgment from others.

Avoidance-oriented goals are goals in which individuals can be negatively motivated to try to avoid failure and to avoid looking incompetent.

For a mastery approach example, Jack›s goal in the class is to learn all of the features of the human body because he is interested in anatomy and physiology and wants to be able to build his base knowledge of these principles.

For a mastery avoidance example, Ashley›s goal in class is to avoid misunderstanding the features of a human body and principles of human physiology as presented to her by her teacher.

For an example of performance approach, Hillary's goal in class is to identify all of the bones, muscles and tissues in the human body more quickly and better than her classmates.

And for performance avoidance, Max's goal in class is to avoid appearing incompetent at identifying anatomy or applying principles of physiology.

It is important to note that students can hold multiple goals simultaneously; thus, it is possible for a student to be both mastery-approach-oriented and performance-approach-oriented. Such a student truly wants to learn and master the material but is also concerned with appearing more competent than others.

WHICH IS BEST? MASTERY OR PERFORMANCE GOALS

Researchers agree that mastery goals are more productive than performance goals, and approach goals are more productive than avoidance goals. Controversy has arisen, however, about whether performance-approach goals should be considered productive and recommended by teachers as a complement to mastery-approach goals.

This four-dimensional perspective of goal orientation led to the multiple-goals perspective in which learners match their goals to their situations and coordinate their goals to pursue multiple goals efficiently and minimize the occurrence of goals that contrast with one another. Researchers assume that students will pursue mastery goals when they value the content and are taught in ways that promote processing strategies, and they will pursue performance goals when there is an emphasis on competition necessary to earn good grades.

MULTIPLE-GOALS DILEMMA

There are concerns with pursuing multiple goals at one time. First, the value of goal coordination is emphasized where students may want to pursue both mastery and performance goals along with social goals, such as pleasing parents and teachers and maintaining social relationships. This can get very complicated and students may worry about the consequences of failure.

RECENT CONCEPTUALIZATIONS

Just over a decade after Dweck conceptualized the two-factor model of goal orientation, VandeWalle proposed that goal orientation is better conceptualized as a three-factor model, further dividing performance goal orientation into the dimensions of avoidant performance goal orientation (APGO) and prove performance goal orientation (PPGO). APGO is centered on the goal of avoiding failure and negative judgment from others centered on lack of competence while PPGO is centered on demonstrating performance to prove competence. Learning goal orientation has also been separated into two categories learning approach orientation and learning avoid orientation, however, this conceptualization is neither widely accepted nor substantially proven. According to VandeWalle, Cron& Slocum, APGO and PPGO have differing relationships with various outcome variables, supporting the argument that a three-factor model should be used in place of the originally conceptualized two-factor model.

GOAL ORIENTATION IN COMMUNICATIONS

In communications there is a theory that coincides with this overall concept. The theory is titled, the Theory of Goal-oriented communications. The idea behind it is that when communicating if individuals are concentrated on the goal at hand rather than the communication itself it will lessen confusion. Communication is not the goal in itself but something bigger, getting a planned idea across.

VANDEWALLE defines learning goal orientation as the "desire to develop the self by acquiring new skills, mastering new situations and improving one's competence" (p. 1000). Persons with learning goal orientation seek feedback on past performance to evaluate current performance. These individuals focus on improving skills and acquiring knowledge, and are less concerned with making mistakes. Research shows that adoption of mastery goals leads to greater intrinsic motivation as opposed to performance approach or performance avoid which are associated with external motivation.

LEARNING-APPROACH AND LEARNING-AVOIDANCE

Although learning goal orientation is most commonly conceptualized as a single construct, researchers have begun to make the approach and avoidance distinction that they have previously done with the performance goal orientation. According to Elliot, learning-approach goals "entail striving to develop one's skills and abilities, advance one's learning, understand material, or complete or master a task". This type of learning goal Orientation is consistent with the way general learning Goal Orientation has been conceptualized previously. Alternatively, learning-avoidance goals "entail striving to avoid losing one's skills and abilities (or having their development stagnate), forgetting what one has learned, misunderstanding material, or leaving a task incomplete"(p. 181). Individuals are likely to pursue learning-avoidance goals when they feel that their skills or abilities are deteriorating. For example, an elderly individual may notice that his/her physical and mental capacity is declining, and as a result may focus his/her goals on sustaining or improving these diminishing capacities.

PROVE PERFORMANCE GOAL ORIENTATION

VandeWalle defines Goal Orientation as the "desire to prove one's competence and to gain favorable judgments about it". The performance approach orientation represents a desire to achieve a high level of performance. Persons with performance approach orientation seek positive reinforcement and feedback. These individuals don't want to put forth a lot of effort unless they will be positively evaluated, and tend to avoid tasks were they may make mistakes and therefore be poorly evaluated.

AVOID PERFORMANCE

VandeWalle defines avoid performance as the "desire to avoid the disproving of one's competence and to avoid negative judgments about it". The performance avoid orientation represents a desire to avoid instances of low believes. Persons with performance avoid orientation focus on avoiding situations in which they will receive evaluations or risk demonstrating lack of confidence. Individuals high in fear of failure are more likely to adopt performance avoid goals.

NEED FOR ACHIEVEMENTS

Need for achievement refers to the degree to which an individual "maintains high standards" and "aspires to accomplish difficult tasks". goal orientation dimensions have been conceptualized as manifestations of Atkinson's (1957) need for achievement and need to avoid failure competence-relevant motives. In a meta-analysis by Payne et al., the authors found that need for achievement was positively correlated with LGO, negatively associated with APGO, and unrelated to PPGO. Another interesting finding by these authors was that need for achievement correlated more strongly with LGO than the trait, conscientiousness. Although LGO and need for achievement were found to be strongly related, the findings demonstrate that LGO is related to, but not synonymous with need for achievement.

ACADEMIC OUTCOMES

Gadamar goal orientation refers to individuals' behavioral tendencies in achievement-oriented tasks. Therefore, it seems intuitive that goal orientation would be associated with various academic outcomes. According to Payne et al., learning goal orientation is positively associated with self-regulatory behaviors such as planning and goal setting, which in turn are associated with academic performance. Thus, individuals with high levels of LGO are more likely to perform well on academic tasks than individuals with high levels of the PGO dimensions. In addition, research has also shown that students' motivation can predict both the quality of the engagement in academic learning as well as the degree to which they seek out or avoid challenging situations. If all students are to move "through the increasing challenges and academic rigors" of school, then their motivation to learn must be identified and nurtured.

ORGANIZATIONAL OUTCOMES

Goal orientation has also been linked to organizational outcomes, specifically job performance. Payne et al. found that individuals with high levels of trait and state LGO and low levels of trait APGO had better job performance. They found that PPGO was unrelated to performance. The authors also found that LGO predicted job performance above and beyond both cognitive ability and the Big Five personality characteristics. This finding suggests that LGO is a valuable predictor of job performance and it may be in the best interest of organizations to create a climate in which learning is valued over performance. In another study by VandeWalle, Cron& Slocum, the authors found that individuals with a learning goal orientation had higher sales performance than those with performance goal Orientations. This finding suggests that in order to be successful in organizational setting, individuals must have the desire to develop their skills

TEMPERAMENT

Temperament refers to those aspects of an individual's personality, such as introversion or extroversion, which are often regarded as innate rather than learned. A great many classificatory schemes for temperament have been developed; none, though, has achieved general consensus in academia (Kagan, 2005).

Historically, the concept of temperament was part of the theory of the four humours, with their corresponding four temperaments.. More recently, scientists seeking evidence of a biological basis of personality have further examined the relationship between temperament and character (defined in this context as the *learnt* aspects of personality). However, biological correlations have proven hard to confirm. (Kagan, 2005)

Temperament is a configuration of observable personality traits, such as habits of communication, patterns of action, and sets of characteristic attitudes, values, and talents. It also encompasses personal needs, the kinds of contributions that individuals make in the workplace, and the roles they play in society.

Each temperament has its own unique qualities and shortcomings, strengths and challenges. To use the idea of Temperament most effectively, it is important to understand that the four temperaments are not simply arbitrary collections of characteristics, but spring from an interaction of the two basic dimensions of human behaviour: our communication and our action, our words and our deeds, or, simply, what we say and what we do.

THURSTONE TEMPERAMENT SCHEDULE (TTS)

Thurstone (1952) states, temperament are concerned with broad personality disposition rather than highly specific acts or traits. The theory suggests seven temperaments, namely, (i) Active, (ii) Vigorous (iii) Impulsive, (iv)Dominant (v) Emotionally stable (vi) Sociable and (vii) Reflective.

Active

Level of activity refers to total energy out. The active person is typically busy and hurry. He likes to keep himself moving. He may seem tireless. His speech and actions are vigorous.

Vigorous

The area emphasizes physical activity using large muscle group and great expenditure of energy. This trait is often described as 'Masculine' but many women and girls will score high in this area.

Impulsive

Impulsivity involves the tendency to respond quickly rather than inhibiting the response. Thetwo main components: 1. resisting versus giving into urges, impulses, or motivational status, and ii. Responding immediately and impetuously to a timulus versus lying back and planning before making a move.

Dominant

Dominant temperament tend to be tall and willowy, with a fast metabolism in youth but often prone to hyper- or hypothyroid conditions as they age. They like efficiency, value their time, and hate to be bored.

Emotionally Stable

Persons who have this trait usually are cheerful and have an even disposition. They can relax in a noisy room, and they remain calm in a crisis. They claim that they can disregard distractions while studying. They are not annoyed by leaving a task unfinished or by having to finish it by deadline.

Sociable

Persons with high score in this area enjoy the company of others, make friends easily and are sympathetic, cooperative and agreeable in their relations with people. Strangers readily approach them about personal troubles.

Reflective

Persons having these traits like meditative and reflective thinking and enjoys dealing with rather than practical problems. Self-examinations are characteristic of reflective persons. These people are usually quiet, work alone and fine detail. They often take on more than they can finish and they would rather plan a job than carry it out.

Personality

Personality can be defined as an individual's unique and relatively stable pattern of behaviour, thoughts and emotions (Robert A. Baron, 1995) .29

Extrovert

One whose interests are directed towards the world around him, who likes people rather than books/ and activity rather than response, and who may often be a salesman or a politician (Henry E. Garret, 1990).

Introvert

It is described as tending to be withdrawn, as primarily interested in his own thoughts and feelings, as seeking solitude and quiet rather than crowds and people, and as being more often than not a solitary or self-sufficient worker. (Henry E. Garret, 1990).

Neuroticism

Neuroticism or emotionality is characterized by high levels of negative affect such as depression and anxiety. Neuroticism, according to Eysenck's theory, is based on activation thresholds in the sympathetic nervous system or visceral brain

Stable

Emotionally stable means exhibiting high activation thresholds and good emotional control, experience negative affect only in the face of very major stressors they are calm and collected under pressure.

THE FOUR TEMPERAMENT TYPES

Each of the four types of humors corresponded in ancient times to a different personality type. These were associated with a domination of various biological functions. Lievegoed suggested that the temperaments come to clearest manifestation in childhood, between approximately 6 and 14 years of age, after which they become subordinate (though still influential) factors in personality.

Sanguine

The sanguine temperament is traditionally associated with air. People with this temperament tend to be lively, sociable, carefree, talkative, and pleasure-seeking. They may be warm-hearted and optimistic. They can make new friends easily, be imaginative and artistic, and often have many ideas. They can be flighty and changeable; thus sanguine personalities may struggle with following tasks all the way through and be chronically late or forgetful.

Pedagogically, they can be best reached through awakening their love for a subject and admiration of people.

Choleric

The choleric temperament is traditionally associated with fire. People with this temperament tend to be egocentric and extroverted. They may be excitable, impulsive, and restless, with reserves of aggression, energy, and/or passion, and try to instill that in others.

They tend to be task-oriented people and are focused on getting a job done efficiently; their motto is usually "do it now." they can be ambitious, strong-willed and like to be in charge. They can show leadership, are good at planning, and are often practical and solution-oriented. They appreciate receiving respect and esteem for their work.

Pedagogically, they can be best reached through mutual respect and appropriate challenges that recognize their capacities.

Melancholic

The melancholic temperament is traditionally associated with the element of earth. People with this temperament may appear serious, introverted, cautious or even suspicious. They can become preoccupied with the tragedy and cruelty in the world and are susceptible to depression and moodiness. They may be focused and conscientious. They often prefer to do things themselves, both to meet their own standards and because they are not inherently sociable.

Pedagogically, they can be best met by awakening their sympathy for others and the suffering of the world.

Phlegmatic

The phlegmatic temperament is traditionally associated with water. People with this temperament may be inward and private, thoughtful, reasonable, calm, patient, caring, and tolerant. They tend to have a rich inner life, seek a quiet, peaceful atmosphere, and be content with themselves. They tend to be steadfast, consistent in their habits, and thus steady and faithful friends.

Pedagogically, their interest is often awakened by experiencing others' interest in a subject.

People of this temperament may appear somewhat ponderous or clumsy. Their speech tends to be slow or appear hesitant.

TITLE OF THE STUDY

"SPIRITUAL INTELLIGENCE IN RELATION TO GOAL ORIENTATION AND TEMPERAMENT AMONG HIGHER SECONDARY STUDENTS"

DEFINITIONS OF TECHNICAL TERMS

Spiritual Intelligence

"Spiritual intelligence as a set of adaptive mental capacities based on non-material and transcendent aspects of reality, specifically those that contribute to the awareness, integration, and adaptive application of the nonmaterial and transcendent aspects of one's existence, leading to such outcomes as deep existential reflection, enhancement of meaning, recognition of a transcendent self, and mastery of spiritual states" (David B. king, 2007)

Goal Orientation

Jose Madapattu (2004) defines academic goals as "motives of an academic nature that students use for guiding their classroom behavior" (in Academic Achievement Goal Orientation:

Temperament

"Character dimensions are consciously learned components of personality which mature in adulthood and influence personal and social effectiveness by insight learning about self-concepts" (Thomas Ollikkunnal2013).

OPERATIONAL DEFINITIONS USED

The three variables selected for the present study are:

1. Spiritual Intelligence
2. Goal Orientation
3. Temperament

The operational definitions of the three variables taken into consideration for the research are:

Spiritual Intelligence

According to the view of the investigator the term "spiritual intelligence" refers to the score obtained by the higher secondary school students on the spiritual intelligence assessment scale constructed by (David b.King 2007)

Goal Orientation

According to the view of the investigator the term "Goal Orientation" refers to the score obtained by the higher secondary school students on the Goal Orientation assessment scale constructed by (Jose Madapattu (2004)

Temperament

According to the view of the investigator the term "Temperement" refers to the score obtained by the higher secondary school students on the temperament assessment scale constructed by (Thomas Ollikkunnal2013)

NEED FOR THE STUDY

The adolescence period is the best time to develop positive emotions and training skills, because adolescents are seeking to find their identity and their future personality at this period. Spiritual intelligence has a significant influence on the quality of life and it goes without saying that adolescence is a sensitive period which requires specific training to make a brighter future and be exposed to the difficulties. Spirituality can be viewed as a form of intelligence because it predicts functioning and adaptation and offers capabilities that enable people to solve problems and attain goals. Conceiving spirituality as a sort of intelligence extends the psychologist's conception of spirituality and allows its association with the rational cognitive processes like goal achievement and problem solving. Emotional intelligence allows people to judge in which situation they are involved and then to behave appropriately within it. Spiritual intelligence allows one to ask if theywant to be in this particular situation in the first place.

SIGNIFICANCE OF THE STUDY

The question raised in the mind of the researcher is whether spiritual intelligence has any relation with Goal Orientation and Temperament. Goal Orientation is a part of motivation and motivation plays a very important role in education. All the theories of learning are based on motivation. A motivated student has a desire to acquire the distinct aim/goal. Goals can be looked at in terms of goal content-what is the desired outcome-and goal processes-what strategies to use to secure the goal. Spiritual intelligence is a new concept introduced in the theory of intelligence. It is important to see the effect of spiritual intelligence on Goal Orientation in students. Now a days it is demand of the time to develop spiritual intelligence among students as they are lacking moral values and aims for preventing violence in educational institutions.

Emmons considers Spiritual Intelligence as a part of intelligence and relates it to goal attainment. Temperament is a part of personality. In education, personality development is given the utmost importance. The aim of teaching is to develop a positive personality of the students. According to Cloninger in spiritual intelligence there is the dimension called "Transcendence" which seems to be directly related to temperament. However, other dimensions like Effectiveness, Cooperativeness, Interpersonal sensitivity, Self-criticism, Self-focused, Social avoidance, Irritability, Personal Reserve, Perfection, Anxious Worrying related to Spiritual Intelligence and its dimensions. The individual spirit with the universal is seen as the ultimate development of human temperament and its ultimate goal. Spiritual intelligence is very important in different walks of life including leaning, perception, creativity a, critically thinking and problem solving etc. therefore the study of spiritual intelligence seems to be relevant to Goal Orientation and Temperament. It seems that Temperament, Goal Orientation and spiritual intelligence are directly or indirectly related to each other in educational field.

OBJECTIVES OF THE STUDY

Every research must have some objectives to achieve. The present study aimed at achieving the following objectives:

1. To find out the level of Spiritual Intelligence along with its dimensions among Higher Secondary School Students.
2. To find out the level of Goal Orientation among Higher Secondary School Students.
3. To find out the level of Temperament along with its dimensions among Higher Secondary School Students
4. To find whether there is any significant difference among Higher Secondary School Students' Critical Existential Thinking, Conscious

State Expansion, Personal Meaning Production and Transcendental Awareness Dimensions of Spiritual Intelligence based on Gender, Medium of Instruction, Type of Management, Type of Family and Family Monthly Income.

5. To find whether there is any significant difference among Higher Secondary School Students' Goal Orientation based on Gender, Medium of Instruction, Type of Management, Type of Family and Family Monthly Income.
6. To find whether there is any significant difference among Higher Secondary School Students' Effectiveness, Cooperativeness, Interpersonal Sensitivity, Self-Criticism, Self-focused, Social Avoidance, Irritability, Personal Reserve, Perfectionism, Anxious Worrying dimensions of Temperament based on Gender, Medium of Instruction, Type of Management, Type of Family and Family Monthly Income
7. To find whether there is any significant correlation among the variables of the study, namely Spiritual Intelligence, Goal Orientation and Temperament of Higher Secondary School Students.

DELIMITATION OF THE STUDY

The present study is delimited into the following aspects:

- This study was conducted among higher secondary school level students.
- The age of the school students selected were between 14 and 18 years.
- The subjects were further classified based on the type of management they belonged to Private, Government and Government Aided
- The Sample was confined to 650.
- The study is conducted only in Chennai educational district.

CONCLUSION

This study has been presented in five chapters. Chapter-1 includes the Introduction of the three variables, Significance of the study, Title of the study, Objectives of the study, Definitions of terms, Delimitations of the study and Organization of the study. Chapter-2 provides a review of literature related to the variables taken in the study. Chapter-3 includes a detailed description of the methodology and strategy for collecting data with a plan for analysis. Chapter-4 is devoted to the presentation and discussion of the analyzed data. Chapter-5 comprises of summary, Implications and suggestion for further research.

❒

2

Review of Literature

The review of related studies involves locating ,studying and evaluating reports of relevant researches and articles, published research abstracts, journals encyclopedias etc. The researcher needs to acquire up to date information about what has been thought and done in a particular area. The researcher draws maximum benefits from the previous investigations, utilizes the previous findings, takes many hints from designs and procedures of previous researchers and formulates an outline for future research. The review of related studies provides the insight into the methods, measures etc. employed by others in the particular area. It provides ideas, theories, explanation, hypotheses of research valuable in formulating and studying the problem at hand. It also furnishes indispensable suggestions related to the problem and already employed techniques to the investigator.

SIGNIFICANCE OF THE STUDY

Research takes the advantage of knowledge which has accumulated in the past as a result of constant human endeavor. It can never be undertaken in isolation of the work that has already been done on the problems which are directly or indirectly related to study proposed by researcher.

A careful review of the researcher journals, books, dissertations, thesis and other sources of information on the problem to be investigated is one of the important steps in the planning of any research study. Review of the related literature, serves the following specific of purposes:

A careful review helps the researcher in selecting the variables lying within the scope of his interest, in defying and operationalizing variables and in identifying variables, which are conceptually and practically important.

1. It helps the researcher in avoiding any duplication of work done earlier.
2. Especially when the stability and validity of its results have been clearly established.
3. It also gives the researcher methodology which refers to the way; the study is to be conducted.
4. The review of the related literature helps the researcher to know about the tools and instruments which proves to be useful and promising in the previous studies.
5. The advantage of the related literature is also to provide insight into statistical methods through which the validity of research is to be established.
6. The final and important specific reason for reviewing the related literature is to know about the recommendations of previous researchers for further research which they have listed in their studies.
7. The researcher has quoted the studies in this chapter that have direct and indirect relevance with the proper study. The studies in this chapter have been classified variable wise as follows:
    - Studies Related To Spiritual Intelligence
    - Studies Related To Goal Orientation
    - Studies Related To Temperament

STUDIES RELATED TO SPIRITUAL INTELLIGENCE

JAIN & PUROHIT (2006) studied the spiritual intelligence of elderly people. For this purpose 200 senior citizens were selected from different living status i.e. living with family (N=100) and living in old age homes (N=100). Findings revealed that no significant difference was found between senior citizens living with family & living in old age homes regarding overall spiritual-intelligence. The findings showed significant differences at many domains of spiritual intelligence such as, GOD and religiosity, soul, self-awareness, interpersonal relations, spirituality in leadership, helping behaviour, flexibility, ability to use and overcome suffering, ability to transcend pain and being spiritually intelligent about death.

DAVID B. KING (2007) defined spiritual intelligence as a set of adaptive mental capacities based on non-material and transcendent aspects of reality, specifically those that: "...contribute to the awareness, integration, and adaptive application of the nonmaterial and transcendent aspects of one's existence, leading to such outcomes as deep existential reflection, enhancement of meaning, recognition of a transcendent self, and mastery of spiritual states." King further proposed four core abilities or capacities of spiritual intelligence: Critical Existential Thinking, Personal Meaning Production, transcendental Awareness, and Conscious State Expansion.

DINCER (2007) discussed spiritual intelligence, the ways to improve spiritual intelligence levels of educators and its positive results on educator-student relationship, and its reflections in the educational environment. They can be the illuminators of tolerance, unity, understanding, love and peace.

AMRAM & DRYER (2008) described in this paper the development and preliminary validation of an ecumenical measure of spiritual intelligence (SI), the Integrated Spiritual Intelligence Scale (ISIS). Spiritual intelligence (SI) was defined as the ability to apply, manifest, and embody spiritual resources, values, and qualities to enhance functioning and wellbeing. ISIS is an 83-item long form, and a 45-item short form, self-report instrument. ISIS has shown satisfactory factor structure, internal consistency, test-retest reliability, and construct validity. It contains 22 subscales assessing separate SI capabilities related to Beauty, Discernment, Egolessness, Equanimity, Freedom, Gratitude, Higher-self, Holism, Immanence, Inner-wholeness, Intuition, Joy, Mindfulness, Openness, Practice, Presence, Purpose, Relatedness, Sacredness, Service, Synthesis, and Trust. These 22 subscales are grouped into 5 domains: Consciousness, Grace, Meaning, Transcendence and Truth. ISIS predicted satisfaction with life and correlated with existing measures of spirituality. ISIS scores were significantly different among the different groups such that spiritual teachers and business leaders were nominated for their embodiment of spirituality in daily life scored higher than other groups such as MBA students, even when controlling for other confounding variables.

AMRAM (2009) investigated contributions of emotional and spiritual intelligences to effective leadership. Participants 42 company CEOs and 210 staff members. Each CEO was administered instruments providing self-reported and 360-degree observer ratings of 5 dimensions of personality, emotional intelligence (EI), and spiritual intelligence (SI). The results suggest that emotional intelligence and spiritual intelligence are distinct constructs, and each contributes to leadership effectiveness. However, relying solely on self-report may not be as robust as a combination of self-report and/or observer ratings of these constructs.

HOWARD ET AL. (2009) defined spiritual intelligence as an interconnected configuration of affective orientations intimately linked to create meaning through connecting ideas, events, and persons rather than to a specific religious tradition or orientation. An exploration of the meaning of transformational leadership in education in K-12 settings provides the basis for the development of a synthesis from a new perspective of two concepts that empower the dispositions of leadership impacting school culture.

LAZAR (2009) examined the relationship between a multidimensional measure of spiritual orientation and measures of psychological functioning among a sample of secular Israeli Jews, one hundred and twelve research participants responded to the Spiritual Orientation Inventory (Elkins et. al., 1988) to self-Report Measures of depression and life satisfaction. Significant relations between total spirituality and both depression and life satisfaction were covered even after controlling for religiousness. Partial Correlations revealed that life coherency, intrinsic values, and experimental aspects of spirituality were related to these measures even after controlling for other dimensions of spirituality. Regression Analysis demonstrated the unique contribution of these three aspects of Spirituality to the prediction of depression and of intrinsic spiritual values to the prediction of life satisfaction.

SAIDY ET AL., (2009) discussed the importance of emotional and spiritual intelligence from the National Education philosophy towards language performance of secondary school students. Five dimensions of emotional intelligence by Goleman Self Awareness, Self-control, motivation, empathy and social skill were discussed and the adaptation suitability of integrated Spiritual Intelligence Scale was discussed for the purpose of measuring spiritual intelligence. The awareness of the needs to enhance secondary students' language skills through emotional and spiritual balance should be given emphasis in the current educational system.

GREEN AND NOBLE (2010) studied that college and university students are curious to explore the questions regarding spirituality through higher education. An integral approach to the study of consciousness addresses this gap by examining theories of consciousness and spirituality from diverse epistemological perspectives, including Western science and non-Western wisdom traditions. This study explored the intellectual and personal effects of this approach for undergraduate students about consciousness .Results showed that students became more open to diverse ideas about consciousness, more self-aware, and more committed to meditation and self-reflection.

HOSSEINI ET AL. (2010) reviewed articles about adolescence, its relation to spiritual intelligence and the related theories. Spiritual intelligence had a significant influence on the quality of life and it goes without saying that adolescence is a sensitive period which requires specific training to make a brighter future and be exposed to the difficulties. Spirituality can be viewed as a form of intelligence because it predicts functioning and adaptation and offers capabilities that enable people to solve problems and attain goals. The results showed that conceiving spirituality as a sort of intelligence extended the psychologist's conception of spirituality and allowed its association with the rational cognitive processes like goal achievement and problem solving. Thus it is concluded that emotional intelligence allowed us to judge in which situation we were involved and then to behave appropriately within it while spiritual intelligence allowed us to ask if we want to be in this particular situation in the first place.

SAGHRAVANI, S. (2010) found that when most people have might ignore other complex applications of their mind. Due to this thought sometimes when people feel that their intelligence is low, that may be disappointed about their abilities and think that their activities may not pull a result.

CHIN ET AL. (2011) studied that organizations require its employees to be more committed as well as to have a better cohesive working interrelationship. Emotional Intelligence is the ability to sense, understand and effectively apply the power and acumen of emotions as a source of human energy, information, connection and influence. Spiritual intelligence is the set of abilities that individuals use to apply, 40 manifest and embody spiritual resources, values and qualities in ways that enhance their daily functioning and well-being. With both these intelligences happening in the workplace, the environment will be more conducive. A better working environment relates to a higher level of productivity.

DANBOLTAB ET AL. (2011) examined religiousness and spirituality in patients with schizophrenia spectrum disorders. Features and subjective significance are described, and associations with psychopathological phenomena are analyzed. The majority of the patients reported that religiousness and spirituality serve a vital positive influence in their ability to cope with their disorder. This positive influence was observed less among those patients with more negative symptoms. The spiritual experience of a divine presence was a common part of spirituality for our respondents, independent of psychopathology, whereas more extraordinary spiritual experiences were associated with certain psychopathological symptoms. Religious patients ruminated less than nonreligious patients did on existential issues, especially regarding the meaning of life, which, together with self-acceptance, was among the key existential issues for these patients.

JELOUDAR ET AL. (2011) analyzed the spiritual intelligence level of teachers employed in government secondary schools in Malaysia, based on selected demographic variables. The sample of the study comprised 203 teachers. The findings of the study showed that there was a significant difference between teachers gender and their spiritual intelligence, but differences were also evident between teachers age groups and their spiritual intelligence. Furthermore, a significant relationship was noted between teachers spiritual intelligence and the six strategies of classroom discipline, including discussion, recognition, involvement, hinting, punishment, and aggression.

MOOSA AND ALI (2011) examined the relationship between parenting styles and spiritual intelligence among high-school students. Results showed that parenting styles can predict spiritual intelligence. Authoritative parenting style had a positive and significant relationship with spiritual intelligence but authoritarian and neglecting parenting styles had negative and significant relationship. Permissive parenting style had no significant relationship.

AYRANCI (2011) studied effects of Top Turkish Managers' Emotional and Spiritual Intelligences on their Organizations' Financial Performance and this study proposed and tested a model that included the possible effects of top Turkish managers' spiritual and emotional intelligences on their organizations' financial performance. Two instruments, the short versions of the Emotional Quotient Inventory (EQ-i:S) and the Integrated Spiritual Intelligence Scale (ISIS), were selected to measure these two forms of intelligence among top managers selected from organizations in the organized industrial zones of Istanbul. The results indicated that some relationships existed among factors related to emotional and spiritual intelligences but that there was not a mixture of 50 these two intelligences. In other words, there was not a common factor that included some of the items of these two forms of intelligence together. Additionally, each of spiritual intelligence factors affected financial performance very weakly, whereas most factors of emotional intelligence did not have any statistically significant effect on the performance. The model showed that the two forms of intelligence combined failed to positively affect financial performance.

HOSSEINI (2010) worked on "A Review Study on Spiritual Intelligence, Adolescence and Spiritual Intelligence, Factors that may Contribute to Individual Differences in Spiritual Intelligence and the Related Theories" and found that the adolescence period is the best time to develop positive emotions and training skills, because adolescents are seeking to find their identity and their future personality at this period. Spiritual intelligence had a significant influence on the quality of life and it goes without saying that adolescence is a sensitive period which requires specific training to make a brighter future and be exposed to the difficulties. Spirituality can be viewed as a form of intelligence because it predicts functioning and adaptation and offers capabilities that enable people to solve problems and attain goals. It was found in the result that conceiving spirituality as a sort of intelligence extended the psychologist's conception of spirituality and allowed its association with the rational cognitive processes like goal achievement and problem solving. Emotional intelligence allowed us to judge in which situation we were involved and then to behave appropriately within it. Spiritual intelligence allowed us to ask if we want to be in this particular situation in the first place.

BABANAZARI ET AL. (2012) investigated the relationship between spiritual intelligence and happiness for Adolescents in High School. The results of the study showed that there was a significant relationship between spiritual intelligence and happiness. Regression analysis showed that awareness sensing, mystery sensing, value sensing and community sensing significantly anticipated happiness.

DOOSTAR (2012) measured spiritual intelligence and surveyed the relationship between spiritual intelligence and organizational citizenship behavior of employees in hospitals and health centers. He also studied the relationship between each of the components of spiritual intelligence and organizational citizenship behavior. The results showed that there was significant relationship between spiritual intelligence and organizational citizenship behavior.

GUPTA (2012) explained the relationship of spiritual intelligence and emotional intelligence with self-efficacy and self-regulation among college students. Wolman's (2001) Psycho matrix Spirituality Inventory (PSI), a 4 point scale, self- reported 49 items questionnaire covering 7 Spiritual factors (divinity, mindfulness, extrasensory perception, community intellectuality, trauma, and childhood spirituality) was used to measure spiritual intelligence of 40 male and 40 female students of Krukshetra University Haryana. Product moment method of correlation and t test were used for data analysis. The findings showed that spiritual intelligence and emotional intelligence were positively and significantly correlated with self- efficacy and self-regulation. Significant difference has been found among male and female students in terms of emotional intelligence, self-efficacy and self-regulation. In the total sample of spiritual intelligence significant difference existed but significant difference did not exist among male and female students in terms of certain dimensions of spiritual intelligence. Males are better in terms of spiritual intelligence, emotional intelligence as comparison to female.

KHADIVI ET AL. (2012) investigated the relationship between spiritual intelligence and self- esteem with students` educational improvement. The results of the study indicated that there was a significant and direct relationship between spiritual intelligence and students` self- esteem. There was no significant relationship between spiritual intelligence and students` educational improvement, however. The study showed that the spiritual intelligence of boys and girls is the same. Girls` self-esteem is more than boys, but boys` educational improvement is more than girls. Also, the results of multiple regression displayed that among the four variables of spiritual intelligence. The spiritual belief, the capability of dealing with problems, self-consciousness, interest, and moral beliefs consisted the 46% of students` self-esteem.

KHOSHTINAT (2012) studied the relationship between spiritual Intelligence and religious coping among the university students Sample size was 400 and applied t test, Pearson correlation test, kai square and logistic correlation tests for analyzing the data. The analysis showed that Spiritual Intelligence and its components namely the existential status of critical thinking; personal interpretation, divine consciousness and transcendental consciousness are significantly higher than average among male and female students.

PRARTHNA (2012) recommended the teaching of emotional and spiritual competencies and values to students for conflict resolution and violence prevention. Conflict resolution and violence prevention programme helps create an open, positive, peaceful campus environment emphasizing tolerance and acceptance of intellectual, cultural as well as religious differences(diversities). Educational Institution should emphasize and inculcate values of love, compassion, empathy, respect, tolerance and peace among students to produce responsible citizens. Spirituality based conflict resolution strategies and principles offers institutions the tools for transforming themselves into true student centered learning community where diversity is seen as strength and conflict is viewed as an opportunity to learn and grow.

SHABANI ET AL. (2012) examined whether, Spiritual Intelligence (SI) and Emotional Intelligence (EI) can be considered as predictor for Mental Health (MH). Also, this study explored the moderating effects of gender on the link between spiritual intelligence and Emotional intelligence with Mental Health among high school students. The participants in the study were 247 high school students, (124 male and 123 female, in the age range between 14-17 years old). The research design was an ex post facto and tested the alternative hypotheses. Three valid and reliable instruments were used to assess, spiritual intelligence Emotional intelligence and Mental Health. Descriptive statistics, multiple and moderated regression analysis were used to analyses the data. The result demonstrated that Mental Health can be influence by spiritual intelligence and Emotional intelligence. In addition, the moderating effect of gender on the relationship of spiritual intelligence and emotional intelligence with Mental Health was not established.

KAUR AND SINGH (2013) studied spiritual intelligence and factor structure underlying Spiritual Intelligence (SI) of prospective engineers and teachers. It was found that there was no significant effect of gender, locality and family status on the factors underlying Spiritual Intelligence except in the domain of extrasensory perception (males> females) and mindfulness (high class> middle class) in case of engineering students and community (middle class> high class), trauma (middle class> high class) and intellectuality (middle class> high class) in case of teacher training students. It was concluded that spiritual intelligence of the students should be enhanced for betterment of society.

STUDIES RELATED TO GOAL ORIENTATION

MIDGLEY ET AL. (1998) made a distinction among conceptually different achievement Goal Orientations including the goal to develop ability (task Goal Orientation), the goal to demonstrate ability (ability-approach Goal Orientation), and the goal to avoid the demonstration of lack of ability (ability-avoid Goal Orientation). The results of studies conducted with seven different samples of elementary and middle school students were used to describe the internal consistency, stability, and construct validity of the scales. Comparisons of these scales with those developed by Nicholls and his colleagues provide evidence of convergent validity. Confirmatory factor analysis attests to the discriminate validity of the scales.

AL-EMADI (2001) tested a model of relations among Goal Orientation, study strategies and achievement. The model postulated that academic achievement and Goal Orientations are related where achievement is related positively to mastery and performance goals but related negatively to avoidance. The mastery goal emerged as a positive predictor of deep processing but a negative predictor of disorganization; the performance goal emerged as a positive predictor of surface processing and deep processing and a negative predictor of disorganization. The performance avoidance goal was posited as a positive predictor of disorganization, but a negative predictor of deep processing and surface processing. As predicted, the mastery goal was a positive predictor of deep processing, the performance goal was a positive predictor of surface processing and avoidance was a positive predictor of disorganization. Achievement was a positive predictor of both surface processing and disorganization.

JAGACINSKI & DUDA (2001) examined three popular measures of task and ego achievement Goal Orientations in terms of factorial and construct validity, internal consistency reliability, and distributional temperament istics. College students completed the ability and Task Orientation scales from the Patterns of Adaptive Learning Survey, Task and Ego Motivational Orientation Scales, and the General Learning and Performance Goal Orientation Scales. The results showed that the first two sets of scales assessed Goal Orientations for schoolwork, whereas the third is more general. To assess construct validity, the scales were correlated with the Jackson Achievement Orientation Scale, beliefs concerning the role of effort and ability in success, and interest/ enjoyment of and boredom with schoolwork. The PALS scales generally faired the best in terms of distributional temperament istics, factorial validity, and construct validity.

ARIAS (2004) analyzed the classic and reformulated versions of Goal Orientation theory looking at assumptions, empirical evidence, inconsistencies and research developed along both lines of study. Finally it evaluated implications in carrying some of these insufficiently verified principles into educational practice.

ESCRIBE and HUET (2005) examined how the accessibility of knowledge and achievement goals affects the maintenance of a categorization strategy, recall performance and perception of the strategy among human science university students in France. The results showed that learning goal promoted maintenance of the categorization strategy and perception of its utility while performance goals only maintained this strategy & perceptions.

MATTERN (2005) compared the achievement patterns of students who held both goals simultaneously to students who held either mastery or performance goals only. Data was collected within a foundational teacher education course from 143 students, a portion of whom were found to hold high mastery goals (mastery oriented), high performance-approach goals (performance-approach oriented), and high mastery and high performance goals (multiple Goal Orientation. A significant difference was found between the high mastery group and the high performance group.

ANDRIESSEN ET AL. (2006) studied future goal setting, task motivation and learning of minority and non-minority students in Dutch schools. The sample consisted of 279 minority students (Turkish and Moroccan origin) and 229 non-minority (native Dutch) students of secondary schools. Task motivation and adaptive learning emerged as the influential predictors of both minority and non-minority students. Future goals were strongly related to more task motivation and indirectly to more adaptive learning strategies.

Was (2006) attempted to include self-implicit theories of intelligence in a measure designed to capture the basic distinctions between mastery, performance approach, performance avoidance and work avoidance Goal Orientations. The results showed the inclusion of self-implicit theories of intelligence in achievement Goal Orientation was necessary. This perception may be fundamental to the way students approach achievement tasks in academic settings.

LEONDARI & GONIDA (2007) studied the relationship between academic self-handicapping, Goal Orientation (task, performance-approach, and performance avoidance), social goals, future consequences and achievement in mathematics. Participants were 702 upper elementary, junior and senior high school girls and boys students. On the total sample self-handicapping was positively related to performance Goal Orientations and negatively to achievement in mathematics. Hierarchical regression analysis showed that the association between achievement in mathematics and self-handicapping was mediated by performance-avoidance goals in upper elementary and junior high schools. Task Goal Orientation was a negative predictor of self-handicapping in senior high school.

CHOUINARD ET AL. (2007) studied the relations between competence beliefs, utility value and achievement goals in mathematics among secondary school students. Results showed that mastery emerged as the influential predictor on students' effort in learning of mathematics. Competence beliefs, utility value, achievement goals and effort were not significantly influenced by age and gender in mathematics.

ROEBKEN (2007) examined the relationship between student Goal Orientation and student satisfaction, academic engagement, and achievement. Using data on 2309 college students from the University of California Undergraduate Experience Survey (UCUES), this study analyzed the relationship between different types of Goal Orientations and student behavior and academic outcomes and explored how students can be classified according to their Goal Orientation, how multiple achievement goals relate to different socio-demographic temperament is tics and the relative influence of Goal Orientation on indices of satisfaction, achievement, and academic engagement among undergraduate students were assessed. The results supported the notion that students pursuing both mastery and performance goals were more satisfied with their academic experience, show a higher degree of academic engagement, and achieve better grades than students who pursue a mastery orientation alone or a work avoidance / performance orientation. One practical implication of the study of Goal Orientation is that student applicants could be screened on the basis of both a high mastery as well as a high performance orientation.

HARRIS ET AL. (2008) investigated the influence of mastery and performance goals on the nature of children's collaborative participation while playing a programme solving computer game with a peer. The findings showed that children who were assigned mastery goals engaged in significantly more collaborated problem solving discussion whilst children who were assigned performance goals engaged in more executive help seeking and displayed lower levels of metacognitive control.

PHAN (2008) studied the impact of the classroom climate and how this psychosocial milieu may influence students' engagement in achievement goals and reflective thinking practice in learning. The result showed that the predictive effects of different facets of the classroom learning environment on mastery and performance (approach, avoidance) goals, and the four phases of reflection. Mastery and performance (approach & avoidance) goals also exerted direct effects on the four phases of reflection .The antecedents of academic performance included students' involvement and performance approach goals. Psychosocial milieu of the classroom contributes to students' achievement Goal Orientations and their engagement in reflective thinking practice.

CANO AND BERBEN (2009) aimed to explore the relationship between Students' approaches to learning and achievement goals to identify subgroups of students with multiple achievement goals and differences between these subgroups with respect to various Students' approaches to learning and achievement goals temperament istics. Students' approaches to learning and achievement goal variables were moderately associated and related to both the way students perceived their academic environment and the way they conceived of the nature of mathematics. Differences were analyzed, between subgroups and attributed them to various constructs including perceptual cognitive framework, learning approaches, and academic performance. The study revealed a consistent pattern of relationships between Students' approaches to learning and achievement goal perspectives across different methods of analysis.

MUIS ET AL. (2009) studied traditional psychometric and modern Rasch-model analyses of the Achievement Goals Questionnaire (AGQ) and the Patterns of Adaptive Learning Scale (PALS) for the assessment of Goal Orientation achievement. Rasch analyses revealed that estimates of reliability for items were very good but respondent ability estimates varied from poor to good for both the AGQ and PALS. These findings indicate that items validly and reliably reflect a group's aggregate Goal Orientation, but using either instrument to temperament is an individual's Goal Orientation is hazardous.

MEYER ET AL. (2009) investigated interrelationships between self-reported motivation orientations and achievement outcomes on the National Certificate on Educational Achievement (NCEA), a standard-based, criterion-referenced assessment system for senior secondary students. Results using factor analyses and regression analysed revealed that several theoretically meaningful self-reported motivation orientations were strongly related to actual achievement including (high achievement) and (low achievement).

PHAN (2009) proposed and tested a conceptual model of relationships among Future Time Perspective (FTP), esp. beliefs, achievement goals (mastery,

Performance Approach, Performance Avoidance), Study processing strategies and academic performance. Results showed that no gender differences in the five theoretical frameworks or academic performance.

LIU ET AL. (2009) identified students' achievement goal profiles at an intra-individual level. Cluster analysis was performed to identify distinct subgroups of students with similar achievement goal profiles. The result indicated that clusters with high achievement goals and clusters with moderately high goals had the most positive psychological temperament is tics and perceived outcomes.

DISETH AND KOBBELTVEDT (2010) investigated the relationship between achievement motives, achievement goals, learning strategies and academic achievement in a hierarchical model. The result showed that academic achievement (examination grade) was positively correlated with performance-approach goal, mastery goal, and strategic learning strategies, and negatively correlated with performance-avoidance goal and surface learning strategy. A path analysis (structural equation model) showed that achievement goals were mediators between achievement motives and learning strategies, and that strategic learning strategies mediated the relationship between achievement goals and academic achievement.

CIANIET AL. (2011) used self-determination theory (SDT) to understand why students enter classes with particular achievement goal profiles. Results indicated that students' autonomy and relatedness need satisfaction in life predict their initial self-determined class motivation, which in turn predicts initial mastery – approach and avoidance goals and perceived teacher autonomy support buffered against the general decline in students' mastery-approach goals over the course of the semester.

SCHWINGER & STIENSMEIER (2011) studied the relationship between students' perceptions of classroom goals and their endorsement of personal achievement goals (i.e.) their perception of mastery, performance-approach, and performance-avoidance goals in the classroom. Through hierarchical linear modeling (HLM) analysis all three classroom goals showed unique associations with students' personal goal adoption. The findings suggested that multiple classroom goals have interactive effects on students' personal achievement strivings.

SVANUM AND AIGNER (2011) examined the within course relations of a set of variables often implicated as potential contributors to the grade-student rating relation. Measures of course mastery and performance goals, expected grades, course effort, cumulative GPA, and final course grade were prospectively collected. Result indicated that all variables predicted course satisfaction, Grades had a moderately strong effect and students high on mastery course goals evaluated the course more positively whereas students high on performance goals provided less favourable evaluations.

KHAIRI ET AL. (2012) aimed at finding the effects of type of sport, gender, personality and Goal Orientation on the sport ethics of student athletes. 399 student athletes (including 208 females and 191 male) from 11 universities participated in this study. The participants were selected through cluster sampling method. They were representatives of all university students all over the country. The final aim of the present research was to design a model based on drawing the path of the effect of the predictive variables of type of sport, gender, personality and Goal Orientation (as the internal independent variable) on sport ethics (criterion variable). The model's hypotheses were tested by analyzing the data collected through a questionnaire which included four subscales as well as through multivariate regression method. The results showed that personality had significant direct and indirect effects on the levels of sport ethics of the student athletes (through Goal Orientation) (" = 0.05). Gender was only affected indirectly through Goal Orientation; however, (individual/team) type of sport had no effect on the levels of sport ethics.

SENKO ET AL. (2012) tested the hypothesis that students pursuing mastery goals favour instructors who stimulate and challenge them intellectually, whereas those pursuing performance goals favour instructors who present material clearly and provide clear cues about how to succeed. The result showed that mastery goals predicted greater demand for professors who intellectually challenge students and possess topic expertise, whereas performance goals predicted high demand for professors who present material clearly and provide clues about how to succeed in the course

STUDIES RELATED TO TEMPERAMENT

CALABRESE AND ROBERTS (2002) described temperament at the core of leadership. Leaders with virtuous temperament provide benefits to their schools and communities whereas; the leaders with temperament flaws create harm for themselves as well as for their community. The ethical lapses among teachers, principals and superintendents create an even larger issue when one considers the fiduciary trust placed in educators by the public temperament development requires behavior change as well as knowledge acquisition. Incorporate behavior changes into university administrator preparation programs require faculty to consider as how the findings in neuroscience as how the brain learns and the incorporation of these findings into program design and instruction.

GILLESPIE ET AL. (2003) studied to determine whether Cloninger's revised 7 factor model of personality showed incremental validity over his four dimensions of temperament. A sample of 2517 Australian twins aged over 50 between 1993 and 1995 returned completed self-reported measures of Self-directedness, Cooperativeness, and Self-transcendence from Cloninger's Temperament and character Inventory. Many of these twins had participated in a 1988 study containing Cloninger's temperament measures of Harm Avoidance, Novelty Seeking, Reward Dependence and Persistence. Contrary to theoretical expectations, univariate analyses revealed that familial aggregation for the temperament dimensions could be entirely explained by additive gene action alone. Although temperament explained 26, 37 and 10% of additive genetic variance in Self-directedness, Cooperativeness and Self-transcendence, respectively, seven genetic factors were required to explain the genetic variance among the TPQ dimensions, and almost all of them on-shared environmental variance was unique to each dimension of temperament . The results indicated that the inclusion of all seven dimensions in taxonomy of personality was warranted.

HARMAN AND DORIS (2003) are of the opinion that experimental studies of human behaviour give good grounds for denying the very existence of moral temperament. This research, according to the authors showed human behaviour to be dependent not on temperament but mainly on one's 'situation'. Herman and Doris developed a number of criticism of this view, among them that social science experiments are ill suited to study temperament, in so far as they do not estimate the role of temperament in continuously shaping the direction of one's life including what situations one is apt to get into the first place.

MARTEINSDOTTIR ET AL. (2003) investigated personality dimensions by means of the Temperament and character Inventory (TCI) in subjects with social phobia with or without a co-existing avoidant personality disorder. Thirty one individuals with social phobia were recruited through advertisement and diagnosed with the structured clinical interview for psychiatric disorder. The social phobia subjects as compared to healthy controls of the same age, scored significantly higher in the TCI dimension measuring harm avoidance but significantly lower in persistence, self-directedness, cooperativeness and self-transcendence. Presence of avoidant personality disorders in the social phobia subjects was associated with significantly higher harm avoidance particularly on the subscale shyness with strangers. In conclusion, individuals with social phobia were temperament sized by high comorbidity of avoidant personality disorders and deviations in TCI personality dimensions. Enhanced harm avoidance was the most prominent personality trait. The observed deviations in TCI dimensions were primarily related to the social phobia itself and not to the presence of concurrent personality disorders.

CARR (2004) discussed that it is a central to virtue ethics both that morally sound action follows from virtuous temperament is itself the product of habitual right judgment and choice that, in short, we choose our moral temperament s. However, any such view may appear to encounter difficulty in those cases of moral conflict where an agent cannot simultaneously act (e.g.) honestly and sympathetically, and in which the choices of agents seem to favour the construction of different moral temperament s. Carr argued against counter arguments, for a view of virtue ethics which embraces the diversity of moral temperament .

BURLEY AND FREIER (2004) described a Gestalt Model of temperament structure and function from the point of view of Gestalt process theory in coordination with E.Tulving's (1985) concept of procedural memory from cognitive and development psychology. Most theories of behaviour and therapy have tended to focus on why behaviours are present. By contrast, the theory and practice of Gestalt therapy has focused primarily on how behaviours are present. Current development research was used to clarify how temperament as an operating system is developed. This conceptual framework permits a description of how temperament functions and how implications for creating change in psychotherapy.

PARKET AL. (2004) investigated the relationship between various temperament strengths and life satisfaction among 5,299 adults from three Internet samples using the Values in Action Inventory of Strengths. Consistently and robustly associated with life satisfaction were hope, zest, gratitude, love, and curiosity. Only weakly associated with life satisfaction, in contrast, were modesty and the intellectual strengths of appreciation of beauty, creativity, judgment, and love of learning. In general, the relationship between temperament strengths and life satisfaction was monotonic, indicated that excess on any one temperament strength does not diminish life satisfaction.

LAPSTEYAND POWER (2005) in the title of their work gave the premise and structure. The central premise is that important insights about temperament and character education will be forthcoming only when there are adequate advances in temperament psychology. How one understanding the moral formation of persons must be conditioned on what we know about personality and development. How we manage the moral education of temperament must be conditioned on what we know about selfhood and identity. They examined critical issues in character psychology, where temperament psychology is understood broadly to include not only psychological literatures that address moral functioning, but also recent trends in ethic that take these literatures seriously as a point of departure for ethic theory. They described the challenge of temperament education in several contexts, including schools, families and sports. And they also identified a number of unifying themes evident among the various chapter along with five prospects for productive interdisciplinary work in chapter psychology and education.

SARROS ET AL. (2005) examined self-assessed temperament among Australian managers in relation to selected demographic variables of these managers, and to establish the initial psychometric properties of the virtuous Leadership Scale used to measure dimensions of temperament. Data were collected through a national online survey of managers utilizing the membership base of the Australian Institute of Management. The findings revealed that self-assessed temperament is multifaceted and varies across specific demographics (gender, age, level of seniority, years as an executive).

GREENWAY ET AL. (2007) described that people use both positive and negative religious coping strategies, and do so in the context of how they perceive their relationship with God, which means that both require individuals to acquire some degree of Self Transcendence. The study attempted to show that Self Transcendence is incorporated in both positive and negative coping strategies. The sample consisted of 190 practicing Anglicans and Catholics. They completed RCOPE from which two variables measuring positive coping and negative coping were then constructed, the Self Transcendence Scale (ST) the item content of which is largely positive and the Spiritual Transcendence Scale (STS) of the Temperament and Temperament Inventory, which acknowledges negative as well as positive experiences. They also completed a scale; God cares, measuring a person's perception of God as caring. In a series of hierarchical regression analyses, all three variables, the perception of God as caring, and both the positive and negative coping variables predicted Self Transcendence and all of its subscales except one. The positive coping variables largely predicted STS, the perception of God as caring variables less so and the negative coping variable not at all. The findings were interpreted as suggesting that both perceiving God as caring and using positive coping strategies limit the problematic feelings associated with negative coping strategies, allowing the Self Transcendence implicit in them to appear.

GREENWOOD (2007) studied the relationship between the positive youth development constructs of temperament and caring with achievement Goal Orientation and ability level variables associated with achievement goal theory in the context of organized American football. Participants were male adolescents attending an intercollegiate football skills camp. The result showed relationship between increased self-reported ability level and the measure of temperament as well as support for an interaction between ability level and orthogonal achievement Goal Orientation on the measure of temperament.

REVELL AND ARTHUR (2007) explored students teacher's attitudes to and experience of temperament and values education in schools and looks at their assessment of the opportunities provided by schools for the development of temperament . The data from over 1000 student teachers in two universities indicated that while they are overwhelmingly in favour of developing their skills in the area of moral development, their opportunities to do this are uneven and are dependent on their course and their teaching placement school. Whilst temperament education is seen as part of citizenship education in the school curriculum in England, the data indicated that it is not part of the formal curriculum of teacher education.

WILHELM (2008) described temperament broadly by leading authorities, including concepts such as practicing apt behavior and teaching right from wrong. Virtue and moral undertones tend to pervade most experts use of temperament, although in secular settings, the notion of ethics is more prominent. Overall, developing in students a desire for the good is how most authorities understand the construct. Implementing temperament in the public and Christian schools, apart from Judeo-Christian view of the construct, leaves schools open to values clarification, situational ethics, and other post-modern foundational options. Temperament development, at least at the conceptual level, is at the heart of all education –Christian or non-Christian.

MEHDI & JORG (2009) investigated relationships between temperament, temperament, and anger experience, control, and expression. The Temperament and Temperament Inventory, the Symptom Checklist 90-R, and the State Trait Anger Expression Inventory were completed by 103 Police trainees. Personality scores were of greater significance compared to SCL-90-R scores for most of the STAXI-2 subscales while the scores of both personality and mental health contributed by a similar amount to trait anger. Temperament subscales explained a much greater amount of anger expression-in variance while variance of temperament subscales explained more of the variance in anger V, angry reaction, state, and trait anger. Temperament was found to be superior to temperament in the determination of anger, supporting a cognitively focused definition of anger.

CLONINGER (2011) studied how well personality accounts for health's affective aspects (i.e., "happiness") and its non-affective aspects (i.e., "wellness") in the general population. 1102 volunteer representatives of the Sharon area of Israel completed the Temperament and character Inventory (TCI), the Positive and Negative Affect Scale (PANAS), the Satisfaction with Life Scale (SWLS), the Multidimensional Scale of Perceived Social Support (PSS), and the subjective health assessment of the General Health Questionnaire (GHQ). Multidimensional personality profiles were used to evaluate the linear and non-linear effects of interactions among dimensions on different aspects of well-being. The results showed that Self-directedness was strongly associated with all aspects of well-being regardless of interactions with other dimensions. Cooperativeness was strongly associated with perceived social support, and weakly with other aspects of well-being, particularly when Self directedness was low. Self-transcendence was strongly associated with positive emotions when the influence of the other temperament dimensions was taken into account. Personality explained nearly half the variance in happiness and more than one-third of the variance in wellness. The emotional, social, and physical aspects of well-being are interdependent, but specific configurations of TCI Self-directedness, Cooperativeness, and Self-transcendence influence them differentially. Interactions among different combinations of temperament traits have strong effects on the perception of both wellness and happiness.

TOP (2012) explored whether temperament education has an impact on preventing school violence through the virtues that it provides, and whether temperament education influences the achievement of children in schools. Temperament education has been a valuable asset in prevention-based strategies. Prevention education is the key in addressing school violence (Miller, Kraus, &Veltkamp, 2008). It has been posited that there is a need to educate students about temperament education through curricular programs in order to create safe and effective academic learning environments (Colorado State Department of Education, Denver, 2000; Robelen, 2001). In addition, researchers have identified the negative relation between violence and moral education.

AHMAD & GHOSH (2012) conducted a comparative study related with moral values, social maturity and life satisfaction amongst male and female college students. The findings revealed that the college students do not differ significantly in Moral Value, Social Maturity and Life Satisfaction on the basis of Medium of study, Family type, family members, fathers' and mothers' education.

WOOD (2012) studied 20 elementary schools in Hawaii and found that a program to build social, emotional and temperament skills resulted in significantly improved quality of education .The program, which is centered on activities to build temperament, only takes about an hour a week away from traditional education, but has led to fewer suspensions, lower absenteeism, and better reading and math scores on standardized tests. The new trend, called social-emotional and temperament development, involves teacher and staff training, parent and community involvement, and continued positive reinforcement. Lessons include topics related to self-concept, physical and intellectual actions, managing oneself responsibly, getting along with others, being honest, and self-improvement.

PSYCHOLOGISTS AT THE UNIVERSITY OF EDINBURGH (2012) studied of more than 800 sets of twins found that genetics were more influential in shaping key traits than a person's home environment and surroundings and said that genetically influenced temperament is tics could well be the key to how successful a person is in life. A series of questions were used to test how they perceived themselves and others. The results were measured according to the Ryff Psychological Well-Being Scale which assessed and standardized these temperament is tics. The research team found that identical twins -- whose DNA is exactly the same -- were twice as likely to share traits compared with non-identical twins. According to Psychologists the findings were significant because the stronger the genetic link, the more likely it is that these temperament traits are carried through a family. It was also found that genetic influence was strongest on a person's sense of self-control. Researchers found that genes affected a person's sense of purpose, how well they get on with people and their ability to continue learning and developing.

SETHI ET AL. (2012) studied in this article the role of morality and spirituality for temperament building. It articulated the spiritual principle and its rationale. It looked at the development of the human condition in the light of spiritual principles. It proposed a way of moral living as a means of identifying an individual human spirit with the universal spirit. Merging of the individual spirit with the universal is seen as the ultimate development of human temperament and its ultimate goal. After collecting the related literature for all the three variables from different journals, books, encyclopedia and websites, the researcher has now come to a valid conclusion that as far as Spiritual Intelligence is concerned it is relatively a new concept and little work has been done on it. Now a days it is demand of the time to develop spiritual intelligence among students as they are lacking moral values and aims for preventing violence in educational institutions.

EMMONS (2000A, 2000B) considers Spiritual Intelligence as a part of intelligence and relates it to goal attainment. According to Esquith (2003) Academic achievement is bond to critical thinking skills (a sub dimension of Spiritual Intelligence). Goal Orientation is a very important variable in educational field. Goal theory originated early in the 20th century but became a particularly important theoretical framework in the study of academic motivation after 1985.Goal Orientation theory examines the reasons why students engage in their academic work. Nearly two decades of research from about 1985 into the early 2000s on achievement Goal Orientations offered educators a number of practical implications for classrooms. As educators think more critically about the types of goals that teachers and schools foster in their students, they may be better able to shape the motivational patterns adopted by children and adolescents in school settings.

Temperament has been a topic of discussion from time immemorial (Sabini& Silver, 1998) found an aesthetic and moral basis of temperament. Calabrese & Roberts (2002) described temperament at the core of leadership. Leaders with virtuous temperament provide benefits to their schools and communities. Greenwood (2007) studied the relationship between the positive youth development constructs of temperament and caring with achievement Goal Orientation and ability level variables associated with achievement goal theory.

SETHI ET. AL (2012) looked the development of the human condition in the light of spiritual principles. Therefore researcher has made a modest attempt to understand the relationship among all these variables Spiritual Intelligence, Goal Orientation and Temperament. Also the researcher is concerned with finding out the multiple regression analyses and differences among these variables. Moreover all the three variables are very important in the present educational setting so how far are they related with each other may prove to be a novel research according to the researcher.

The researcher has taken these variables in the present study. Goal Orientation and Temperament are for long accepted as part of educational aims. The researcher in the present study has taken Goal Orientation and Temperament as independent variables. Spiritual Intelligence is relatively a new concept and it has been treated as dependent variable in the present study.

CONCLUSION

Reviewing the literature showed that, spiritual intelligence can improve with training. Adolescence is an important period for spiritual intelligence training and gratitude as a subscale in SQ has ability to increase that fortunately, many individuals have described specific exercises to promote gratitude. As a sort of intelligence, spirituality extends the psychologist's conception of spirituality and allows its association with rational cognitive processes like goal achievement and problem resolution. The spiritual intelligence provides a general basis for the individual to be able to consider his seeking for goals and meaning in life, and to move in the direction of the aims which are personally meaningful. It aids the individual in directing his/her concerns to the wider image and in focusing, consciously, his/her activities in a context that is wider.

❐

3

Research Design and Methods of Investigation

Research methods are of almost Importance in research process. They describe the various plans of attach to be adopted in solving research problem such as the manner in which the problems are formulated, the definition of terms, the choice of subjects for investigation, the validation of data gathering tools, the collection analyze and interpretation of data. The process of interference and generalization.

ACCORDING TO CLAIRE SELLTIZ,

A research design is the arrangement of condition for collection and analyze of data in a manner that aims to combine relevance to the research purpose with economic in procedure.

ACCORDING TO THYER,

The research design is about print for new research study is to be completed operations listing variables so they can be measured selecting a sample of interest to study, collecting data to be used as a basic for testing hypothesis and analyzing the results.

NEED FOR RESEARCH DESIGN

Research design facilitates the smooth sailing of the various research operation, thereby making research as efficient as possible, yielding maximal information with minimal expenditure of effort, time and money. We need a research design or a plan in advance of data collection and analysis for our research project.

Research design stands for advance planning of the methods to be adopted for objectives of the research and the availability of staff, time and money preparation of the design should be done with great care, as any error may upset the entire project. Research design in fact, has a great bearing on the reliability of the results arrived and as such constitute the firm foundation of the entire edifice of the research work.

DESIGN OF THE STUDY

Choosing a design for a study basically involves selecting the most appropriate technique to solve the particular problem under investigation Anerson, Durston& Poole (1970).

HYPOTHESES OF THE STUDY

A hypothesis is a tentative generalization and is the basis for investigation.

According to **Carter V Good,** A hypothesis is a shrewd guess or inference that is formulated and provisionally adopted to explain observed factors or conditions and to guide in further investigation.

HYPOTHESIS OF THE STUDY

1. The levels of Spiritual Intelligence along with its dimensions among Higher Secondary School Students are moderate in nature.
2. The level of Goal Orientation among Higher Secondary School Students is moderate in nature.
3. The levels of Temperament along with its dimensions among Higher Secondary School Students are moderate in nature.
4. There is no significant difference among Higher Secondary School Students' Spiritual Intelligence and its dimensions (Critical Existential Thinking, Personal Meaning Production, Transcendental Awareness and Conscious State Expansion) based on Gender, Medium of Instruction, Type of Management, Type of Family, and Family Monthly Income.
5. There is no significant difference among Higher Secondary School Students' Goal Orientation based on Gender, Medium of Instruction, Type of Management, Type of Family and Family Monthly Income.
6. There is no significant difference among Higher Secondary School Students' **Temperament** and its dimensions (Effectiveness,

Cooperativeness, Interpersonal sensitivity, Self-criticism, Self-focused, Social avoidance, Irritability, Personal reserve, Perfectionism and anxious worrying) based on their Gender, Medium of Instruction, Type of Management, Type of Family and Family Monthly Income.

7. There is no significant correlation between Spiritual Intelligence and Temperament among Higher Secondary School Students.
8. There is no significant correlation between Spiritual Intelligence and Temperament among Higher Secondary School Students.
9. There is no significant correlation between Goal Orientation and temperament among higher secondary school students.

TOOLS AND TECHNIQUES USED

To verify the hypotheses formulated in the study, the following tools have been used.

1. Spiritual Intelligence questionnaire constructed by David. King in the year 2008.
2. Goal Orientation inventory was constructed by José Maddapattu. in the 2010.
3. Temperament scale was constructed by Thomas Ollikunnalin the year 2014.

SPIRITUAL INTELLIGENCE SCALE

Description

In order to measure the spiritual intelligence of higher secondary students, spiritual intelligence questionnaire designed by **King. D**in the year 2008 has been used. This test consists of 24 statements which are designed to measure various behaiours, thought processes and mental characteristics. And for each statements six alternatives five alternative answers are given (not at all true of me, not very true of me, somewhat true of me, very true of me, completely true of me)

Administration

The students were asked to read instructions carefully and make their responses by putting a tick (√) mark against the choices provided. They were assured that there were no right or wrong choices for the questions.

SCORING PROCEDURES OF SPIRITUAL INTELLIGENCE

24 items in total; range: 0-96

4 Factors/Subscales

1. Critical Existential Thinking (CET)

- Sum Items 1, 3,5,9,13,17, and 21.
- 7 items in total; range: 0-28

2. Personal Meaning Production (PMP):

- Sum items 7,11,15,19, and 23.
- 5 items in total; range: 0 – 20

3. Transcendental Awareness (TA):

- Sum items 2, -6, 10,14,18,20, and 22.
- 7 items in total; range 0-28

4. Conscious State Expansion (CSE):

- Sum items 4, 8, 12, 16, and 24.
- 5 items in total; range: 0-20

Reverse coding: item – 6 (response must be reversed prior to summing scores).

Higher scores represent higher levels of spiritual intelligence and / or each capacity.

GOAL ORIENTATION SCALE

Description

In order to measure the Goal Orientation of Higher Secondary Students, Goal Orientation questionnaire constructed by Jose Maddapattu in the year 2010 is used. Goal Orientation survey is consisting of 7 statements each statement has five point answer maximum score is 35 and minimum is 0.

ADMINISTRATION

Goal Orientation – teen survey is administered to higher secondary school students.

SCORING

Each item was accorded a five point response score; the intervals of which was labelled as

- Not at all like me
- A little like me
- Somewhat like me
- A not like me
- Exactly like me are the responses for first five statements.

For other statements responses are

- None of the time
- A little of the time
- Some of the time
- Most of the time

- All of the time

The successive response intervals subsequently were scorec as 5,4,3,2 & 1 where the high score represents higher Goal Orientation. The answers were checked against the key and points were given for each item and ticked as per the key. The total points obtained gave a measurable of Goal Orientation.

TEMPERAMENT INVENTORY SCALE

Description

In order to measure the temperament of higher secondary students, temperament scale which was constructed by Thomas Ollikunnalin the year 2014 was used. This test consists of 50 statements.

Positive statements	1,2,3,4,5,6,8,9,10,12,13,14,15,21,22,23,24,25,41,42,43,44,45,46
Negative statements	7,11,16,17,18,19,20,26,27,28,29,30,31,32,33,34,35,36,37,38,39,40,47,48,49,50.

1. **Effectiveness**
   - Sum items; 1,2,3,4, and 5
   - 5 items in total; range 5-25
2. **Cooperativeness**
   - Sum items; 6,-7, 8, 9 and 10
   - 5 items in total; range 5-25
3. **Interpersonal sensitivity**
   - Sum items; -11, 12, 13, 14 and 15
   - 5 items in total; range 5-25
4. **Self-Criticism**
   - Sum items; -16,-17,-18,-19 and -20
   - 5 items in total; range 5-25
5. **Self-focused**
   - Sum items; 21,22,23,24 and 25
   - 5 items in total; range 5-25
6. **Social avoidance**
   - Sum items; -26,-27,-28,-29 and -30
   - 5 items in total; range 5-25

7. Irritability

- Sum items; -31,-32,-33,-34 and -35
- 5 items in total; range 5-25

8. Personal Reserve

- Sum items; -36,-37,-38,-39 and -40
- 5 items in total; range 5-25

9. Perfection

- Sum items; 41,42,43,44 and 45
- 5 items in total; range 5-25

10. Anxious Worrying

- Sum items; 46,-47,-48,-49 and -50
- 5 items in total; range 5-25

SCORING PROCEDURE USED FOR MEASURE THE TEMPERAMENT OF HIGHER SECONDARY SCHOOL STUDENTS

Response	Positive	Negative
Not true at all	1	4
Slightly true	2	3
Moderately true	3	2
Very true	4	1

SAMPLE OF THE STUDY

To cover the entire population is practically an impossible task for any sutvey or research. What is feasible and generally practiced is to study a sample representative of the population.

The aim of sampling is to choose a subset in a way that will serve as adequate representative of population as a whole **(Weiss 1968)**. Thus, validity of the result obtained is dependent in part, upon adequacy and representatives of population **(Freeman 1963)**.

Therefore, a sample of 650 cases had been drawn by stratified random sampling for the present study. The sample consisted of both males and females.

Higher secondary school students from Government, Government Aided and Private schools were taken as sample. The sample selected for study is shown in the table below.

DISTRIBUTION OF THE SAMPLE

S.No	Name of the school	Sample size
1	St. Bed's Anglo Indian Higher Secondary School	50
2	Egmore Don Bosco Higher Secondary School	50
3	St. Mary's Anglo Indian higher Secondary School	50
4	Bon Secures Higher Secondary School	50
5	Rosary Matriculation Higher Secondary School	50
6	St. Joseph's Higher Secondary School	50
7	Hindu Higher Secondary School	60
8	Chennai Boy's Higher Secondary School	80
9	Chennai Girls Higher Secondary School	50
10	Government Girls Higher Secondary School	60
11	Government Higher Secondary School for Girls	50
12	Wesley higher secondary school	50
	Total	**650**

PILOT STUDY

Before finalizing the final form of the tools and collecting data for main study, a pilot study was attempted in November 2014. It was conducted among hundred higher secondary school students to establish reliability and validity of the tools used in the study.

RELIABILITY OF THE TOOLS

The reliability of a test may be defined as the degree of consistency with which the test measures what it does measures. A test score is called reliable when we have reasons to believe it to be stable and trust worthy. The reliability of the different tools used for the present study were established as follows.

RELIABILITY OF SPIRITUAL INTELLIGENCE

In the study, the tool was administered for its reliability by the split – half technique. It was done by using Spearman – Brown formula.The reliability of spiritual intelligence was found to be (.94) the spiritual intelligence inventory was considered to be highly reliable.

RELIABILITY OF GOAL ORIENTATION

The index of validity which is the square root of reliability was found to be (0.78) and it is found to be highly valid.

RELIABILITY TEMPERAMENT

In order to establish the reliability of the temperament inventory, the odd-even method was used. The reliability of temperament was found to be (.93) the temperament inventory was considered to be highly reliable.

VALIDITY OF THE TOOLS

A test is said to be valid, if it measures only what it intends to measure. In other words, it could be said "A test is valid, when the performance which it measures corresponds to the same performance as otherwise independently measured or objectively measures."

VALIDITY OF THE SPIRITUAL INTELLIGENCE

The index of validity which is the square root of reliability was found to be (0.97) and it is found to be highly valid.

VALIDITY OF THE GOAL ORIENTATION SURVEY

The index of validity which is the square root of reliability was found to be (0.88) and it is found to be highly valid.

VALIDITY OF THE TEMPERAMENT TEST

The index of validity which is the square root of reliability was found to be (0.87) and it is found to be highly valid.

MAIN STUDY

The validated tools were made used for the main study to collect the necessary data. For this, researcher took multiple copies of the tools of the study and circulated to the higher secondary school students in different schools in the month of November 2014.

STATISTICAL TECHNIQUES USED

The investigator uses the following statistical methods to analyze and interpret data.

ARITHMETIC MEAN

$$\text{Mean, } \bar{x} = A + \frac{\sum fd}{\sum f} \times i$$

Where,

A = Assumed Mean

f = Frequency

d = Deviation from the assumed mean

i = Class Interval

FORMULA TO FIND STANDARD DEVIATION (SD)

Standard Deviation, $\sigma = \sqrt{\frac{\sum fd^2}{N} - \left(\frac{\sum fd}{N}\right)^2} \times i$

Where,

f = Frequency

d = Deviation from the arithmetic mean

i = Class Interval

N = Total frequency

FORMULA TO FIND STANDARD ERROR OF MEAN DIFFERENCE

Standard Error Deviation, SED = $\sqrt{\frac{\sigma_1^2}{N_1} + \frac{\sigma_2^2}{N_2}}$

Where,

$\sigma_{1,}\ \sigma_2$ = Standard deviations

N_1, N_2 = Total number of sample

FORMULA TO FIND OUT "t" VALUE

To find out the significant difference between two means, we use 't'

t - Ratio = $\frac{M_1 \sim M_2}{\sqrt{\frac{\sigma_1^2}{N_1} + \frac{\sigma_2^2}{N_2}}}$

Where,
M_1, M_2 = means of the group.
$\sigma_{1,}\ \sigma_2$ = Standard deviations
S_{ED} = Standard error deviation
N_1, N_2 = Total number of sample

FORMULA TO FIND COEFFICIENT OF CORRELATION

$$r = \frac{N\sum x\sum y - \sum x\sum y}{\sqrt{\left(N\sum x^2 - \left(\sum x^2\right)\right)\left(N\sum Y^2 - \left(\sum y\right)^2\right.}}$$

x, y – variables

N – Total Strength

CONCLUSION

This chapter outlines the design of the present study, the procedure followed and the nature of the sample. It describes the hypotheses to be tested, the tools used and the methods of administration and scoring. The collected data were analyzed using appropriate statistical techniques described above to study the effect of spiritual intelligence on Goal Orientation and temperament among higher secondary school students, the result of which are discussed in the light of hypotheses formulated and the next chapter presents the analysis and discussion part of the study.

❐

4

Analysis and Interpretation of Data

The result section describes the statistical techniques or the inferential interpretations that were applied to the data, and the results of these analyses. For each hypothesis, the statistical test of significance selected and applied to the data is described, followed by a statement indicating whether the hypothesis was supported or non-supported. Tables present the numerical data are uncluttered and self-explanatory. Charts and diagrams showing the relationships among identified topics, categories and patterns are presented in the result section.

The logic and description of the interpretation linked to qualitative charts and diagrams is an important aspect of qualitative research.

CATEGORIZATION OF THE SAMPLE BASED ON THE VARIABLES OF THE STUDY

CATEGORIZATION OF THE SAMPLE BASED ON SPIRITUAL INTELLIGENCE

Hypothesis-1

The level of Spiritual Intelligence is moderate in nature among Higher Secondary School Students.

TABLE. 4.1: Showing the Distribution and Percentage of Spiritual Intelligence among Higher Secondary School Students

Variable	Level	Frequency	Percentage
Spiritual Intelligence	Low	169	26.0
	Moderate	312	48.0
	High	169	26.0
	Total	650	100.0

From the above table it is clearly observed that majority of the Higher Secondary School Students fall in the moderate level in their Spiritual Intelligence. And thereby the hypothesis is accepted.

CATEGORIZATION OF THE SAMPLE BASED ON GOAL ORIENTATION.

Hypothesis-2

The level of Goal Orientation is moderate in natureamong Higher Secondary School Students.

TABLE. 4.2: Showing the Distribution and Percentage of Higher Secondary Students'Goal Orientation

Variable	Level	Frequency	Percentage
Goal Orientation	Low	176	26.0
	Moderate	300	48.0
	High	174	26.0
	Total	650	100.0

From the above table it is clearly observed that majority of the Higher Secondary School Students fall in the moderate level in their Goal Orientation. And thereby the hypothesis is accepted.

CATEGORIZATION OF THE SAMPLE BASED ON TEMPERAMENT

Hypothesis-3

The level of Temperament is moderate in nature among Higher Secondary School Students.

TABLE. 4.3: Showing the Distribution and Percentage of Higher Secondary Students' Temperament

Variable	Level	Frequency	Percentage
Temperament	Low	169	26.0
	Moderate	299	46.0
	High	182	28.0
	Total	650	100.0

From the above table it is clearly observed that majority of the Higher Secondary School Students; fall in the moderate level in their Temperament. And thereby the hypothesis is accepted.

INFLUENCE OF GENDER ON SPIRITUAL INTELLIGENCE AND ITS DIMENSIONS

Hypothesis-4

There is no significant difference among Higher Secondary School Students' Spiritual Intelligence and its dimensions based on Gender.

TABLE.4.4: Mean, S.D and C.R value for Spiritual Intelligence and its Dimensions classified based on Gender

Variable	Gender	N	Mean	S.D	C.R value	L.S
Critical Existential Thinking	Boys	325	20.08	5.106	2 848	0.01
	Girls	325	18.92	5.276		
Personal Meaning Production	Boys	325	13.00	4.425	0 109	NS
	Girls	325	12.96	4.943		
Transcendental Awareness	Boys	325	20.36	4.764	3 264	0.01
	Girls	325	19.04	5.518		
Conscious State Expansion	Boys	325	13.24	4.382	2 160	0.05
	Girls	325	12.48	4.586		
Spiritual Intelligence (Total)	Boys	325	66.68	16.785	2 380	0.05
	Girls	325	63.40	18.317		

INFERENCE

From the above table, it is observed in the dimensions Critical Existential Thinking and Transcendental Awareness of Spiritual Intelligence, it is found that there is a significant difference at 0.01 levels. And in the dimension conscious state expansion of spiritual intelligence, it is found that there is a significant difference at 0.05 level. Whereas in the dimension Personal Meaning Production of Spiritual Intelligence, it is found that there is no significant difference between Boys and Girls.

However, it is observed in the overall Spiritual Intelligence that the obtained C.R value 2.380 is greater than the table value (1.96) at 0.05, level of significance.

In the dimensions of Critical Existential Thinking, Transcendental Awareness and Conscious State Expansion of Spiritual Intelligence the mean scores reveal that Boys have higher Spiritual Intelligence.

Hence, the null hypothesis is rejected.

INFLUENCE OF MEDIUM OF INSTRUCTIONS ON SPIRITUAL INTELLIGENCE AND ITS DIMENSIONS

Hypothesis-5

There is no significant difference among Higher Secondary School Students' Spiritual Intelligence and its Dimensions based on Medium of Instructions.

TABLE. 4.5: Mean, S.D and t value for Spiritual Intelligence and its Dimensions classified based on Medium of Instructions

Variable	Medium	N	Mean	S.D	C.R value	L.S
Critical Existential Thinking	Tamil	195	15.53	6.423	14.612	0.01
	English	455	21.20	3.416		
Personal Meaning Production	Tamil	195	9.27	4.752	15.456	0.01
	English	455	14.57	3.647		
Transcendental Awareness	Tamil	195	15.67	6.295	15.045	0.01
	English	455	21.43	3.412		
Conscious state Expansion	Tamil	195	10.27	5.399	10.385	0.01
	English	455	13.97	3.519		
Spiritual Intelligence (Total)	Tamil	195	50.73	22.176	15.979	0.01
	English	455	71.17	10.422		

INFERENCE

From the above table, it is observed in the dimensions Critical Existential Thinking, Personal Meaning Production, Transcendental Awareness and Conscious State Expansion of Spiritual Intelligence; it is found that there is a significant difference at 0.01 levels.

It is observed in the overall Spiritual Intelligence that the obtained C.R value 15.979 is greater than the table value (2.58) at 0.01, level of significance.

In the dimensions of Critical Existential Thinking, Personal Meaning Production Transcendental Awareness and Conscious State Expansion of Spiritual Intelligence the mean scores reveal that Tamil Medium Higher Secondary School Students have higher Spiritual Intelligence.

Hence, the null hypothesis is rejected.

INFLUENCE OF TYPE OF MANAGEMENT ON SPIRITUAL INTELLIGENCE AND ITS DIMENSIONS

Hypothesis-6

There is no significant difference among Higher Secondary School Students' Spiritual Intelligence and its dimensions based on Type of Management.

TABLE.4.6: ANNOVA - Showing Significant Difference in Spiritual Intelligence and its Dimensions among Higher Secondary School Students in Relation to Type of Management

Variable	T/M	Sum of squares	Df	Mean square	F	L/S
CET	Between Groups	10495.550	2	5247.775	472.164	0.01
	Within Groups	7190.950	647	11.114		
	Total	17686.500	649			
PMP	Between Groups	7477.990	2	3738.995	356.659	0.01
	Within Groups	6782.750	647	10.483		
	Total	14260.740	649			
TA	Between Groups	10755.550	2	5377.775	515.550	0.01
	Within Groups	6748.950	647	10.431		
	Total	17504.500	649			
CSE	Between Groups	6353.360	2	3176.680	303.282	0.01
	Within Groups	6776.900	647	10.474		
	Total	13130.260	649			
SI (Total)	Between Groups	136240.910	2	68120.455	672.966	0.01
	Within Groups	65492.050	647	101.224		
	Total	201732.960	649			

INFERENCE

It is inferred from the above table that the Type of Management has a significant influence on the dimensions Critical Existential Thinking, Personal Meaning Production, Transcendental Awareness and Conscious state Expansion of Spiritual Intelligence.

Hence, the null hypothesis is rejected.

To find out the levels of difference further analysis is done and represented in the next table.

TABLE.4.6 (A) Showing mean, S.D and t value for Critical Existential Thinking, the dimension of Spiritual Intelligence among Higher Secondary School Students based on Type of Management

Variable	Type of management	Number of cases	Mean	S.D	C.R value	L.S
Critical Existential Thinking	Private	260	22.30	2.818	32.840	0.01
	Government	130	11.60	3.425		
	Private	260	22.30	2.818	5.682	0.01
	Govt.Aided	260	20.65	3.739		
	Government	130	11.60	3.425	23.160	0.01
	Govt.Aided	260	20.65	3.739		

The above table shows that there is significant difference in the dimension of Critical Existential Thinking of Spiritual Intelligence between Private and Government higher secondary school students, Private and Government Aided higher secondary School Students and Government and Government Aided higher secondary school students.

TABLE.4.6 (B) Showing Mean, S.D and t value for Personal Meaning Production, the dimension of Spiritual Intelligence among Higher Secondary School Students based on Type of Management

Variable	Type of management	Number of cases	Mean	S.D	C.R value	L.S
Personal Meaning Production	Private	260	14.55	4.197	21.272	0.01
	Government	130	6.20	2.190		
	Private	260	14.55	4.197	0.826	NS
	Govt.Aided	260	14.80	2.487		
	Government	130	6.20	2.190	33.468	0.01
	Govt.Aided	260	14.80	2.487		

The above table shows that there is significant difference in the Personal Meaning Production dimension of Spiritual Intelligence between Private and Government higher secondary School Students and Government and Government Aided higher School Students at (0.01) level. And there is no significant difference found between Private and Government Aided higher secondary School Students.

TABLE.4.6 (C) Showing mean, S.D and t value for Transcendental Awareness, and thedimension of Spiritual Intelligence among Higher Secondary School Students based on Type of Management

Variable	Type of management	Number of cases	Mean	S.D	C.R value	L.S
Transcendental Awareness	Private	260	22.15	3.588	29.406	0.01
	Government	130	11.60	2.775		
	Private	260	22.15	3.588	2.907	0.01
	Govt.Aided	260	21.30	3.057		
	Government	130	11.60	2.775	30.444	0.01
	Govt.Aided	260	21.30	3.057		

The above table shows that there is significant difference in the Transcendental Awareness, a dimension of Spiritual Intelligence between Private and Government higher secondary School Students, Private and Government Aided School Students and Government and Government Aided higher secondary School Students at (0.01) level.

TABLE.4.6 (D) Showing Mean, S.D and t value for Conscious State Expansion, the dimension of Spiritual Intelligence among Higher Secondary School Students based on Type of Management

Variable	Type of management	Number of cases	Mean	S.D	C.R value	L.S
Conscious State Expansion	Private	260	13.80	3.703	20.466	0.01
	Government	130	6.70	1.959		
	Private	260	13.80	3.703	3.929	0.01
	Govt.Aided	260	15.00	3.247		
	Government	130	6.70	1.959	26.800	0.01
	Govt.Aided	260	15.00	3.247		

The above table shows that there is significant difference in the Conscious State Expansion, the dimension of Spiritual Intelligence between Private and Government higher secondary School Students, Private and Government Aided School Students and Government and Government Aided higher secondary School Students at (0.01)level.

TABLE.4.6 (E) Showing mean, S.D and t value for Spiritual Intelligence among Higher Secondary School Students based on Type of Management

Variable	Type of management	Number of cases	Mean	S.D	C.R value	L.S
Spiritual Intelligence (Total)	Private	260	72.80	10.042	35.658	0.01
	Government	130	36.10	8.582		
	Private	260	72.80	10.042	1.152	NS
	Govt.Aided	260	71.75	10.739		
	Government	130	36.10	8.582	32.946	0.01
	Govt.Aided	260	71.75	10.739		

The above table shows that there is significant difference in the Spiritual Intelligence between Private and Government School Students and Government and Government Aided School Students at **(0.01)** level. And there is no significant difference found between Private and Government Aided higher secondary School Students.

INFLUENCE OF TYPE OF FAMILY ON SPIRITUAL INTELLIGENCE AND ITS DIMENSIONS

Hypothesis-7

There is no significant difference among Higher Secondary School Students' Spiritual Intelligence and its dimensions based on Type of Family.

TABLE.4.7: Mean, S.D and t value for Spiritual Intelligence and its Dimensions Classified based on Type of Family

Variable	Type of Family	N	Mean	S.D	C.R value	LS
Critical Existential Thinking	Nuclear	442	19.79	5.428	2.099	0.05
	Joint	208	18.88	4.700		
Personal Meaning Production	Nuclear	442	13.00	4.994	0.158	NS
	Joint	208	12.94	3.970		
Transcendental Awareness	Nuclear	442	20.09	5.512	2.793	0.01
	Joint	208	18.88	4.339		
Conscious state expansion	Nuclear	442	12.82	5.049	0.301	NS
	Joint	208	12.94	3.017		
Spiritual Intelligence (Total)	Nuclear	442	65.71	19.120	1.405	NS
	Joint	208	63.63	13.885		

From the above table, it is observed in the dimension Transcendental Awareness of Spiritual Intelligence that there is a significant difference at 0.01 level. And in the dimension Critical Existential Thinking of Spiritual Intelligence, it is found that there is a significant difference at 0.05 level. Whereas in the dimension Personal Meaning Production and Conscious State Expansion of Spiritual Intelligence, it is found that there is no significant difference between Nuclear and Joint Family.

It is observed in the overall Spiritual Intelligence that the obtained C.R value **1.405** is lesser than the table value **(1.96)** at **0.05,** level of significance.

Hence, the null hypothesis accepted.

In the dimensions of Transcendental Awareness and Critical Existential Thinking of Spiritual Intelligence the mean scores reveal that Students who belong to Nuclear Family have Higher Spiritual Intelligence.

INFLUENCE OF FAMILY MONTHLY INCOME ON SPIRITUAL INTELLIGENCE AND ITS DIMENSIONS

There is no significant difference among Higher Secondary School Students' Spiritual Intelligence and its dimensions based on Family Income.

TABLE.4.8: Mean, S.D and t value for Spiritual Intelligence and its Dimensions Classified based on Family Income

Variable	Income	N	Mean	S.D	C.R value	LS
Critical Existential Thinking	Below 15,000	156	12.75	4.298	26.966	0.01
	Above 15,000	494	21.63	3.331		
Personal Meaning Production	Below 15,000	156	7.33	3.459	23.444	0.01
	Above 15.000	494	14.76	3.448		
Transcendental Awareness	Below 15,000	156	12.92	3.938	27.557	0.01
	Above 15,000	494	21.84	3.387		
Conscious State Expansion	Below 15,000	156	8.33	4.123	17.476	0.01
	Above 15,000	494	14.29	3.572		
Spiritual Intelligence (Total)	Below 15,000	156	41.33	14.638	29.419	0.01
	Above 15,000	494	72.53	10.384		

INFERENCE

From the above table, it is observed in the dimensions Critical Existential Thinking, Personal Meaning Production, Transcendental Awareness and Conscious State Expansion of Spiritual Intelligence; it is found that there is a significant difference at 0.01 level.

It is observed in the overall Spiritual Intelligence that the obtained C.R value 29.419 is greater than the table value (2.58) at 0.01 level of significance.

In the dimensions of Critical Existential Thinking, Personal Meaning Production, Transcendental Awareness and Conscious State Expansion of Spiritual Intelligence the Mean Scores reveal that Students' parents who earn more than Rs.15.000, per month have higher Spiritual Intelligence

INFLUENCE OF GENDER ON GOAL ORIENTATION

Hypothesis-9

There is no significant difference among Higher Secondary School Students' Goal Orientation based on Gender.

TABLE.4.9: Mean, S.D and t value for Goal Orientation Classified based on Gender

Variable	Gender	N	Mean	S.D	C.R value	LS
Goal Orientation	Boys	325	21.16	5.342	0.334	NS
	Girls	325	21.00	6.775		

From the above table, it is observed that the obtained Critical Ratio Value **(0.334)** is lesser than the table value **(1.96)** at **0.05,** level of significance. So, it is concluded that there does not exist any significant difference in the Goal Orientation of Higher Secondary School Students based on Gender.

Hence, the null hypothesis is accepted.

INFLUENCE OF MEDIUM OF INSTRUCTION ON GOALORIENTATION

Hypothesis-10

There is no significant difference among Higher Secondary School Students' Goal Orientation based on Medium of Instruction.

TABLE.4.10: Mean, S.D and t Value for Goal Orientation Classified based on Medium of Instruction

Variable	Medium of Instruction	N	Mean	S.D	C.R.value	LS
Goal Orientation	Tamil	195	16.13	6.739	15.975	0.01
	English	455	23.20	4.326		

From the above table, it is observed that the obtained Critical Ratio Value (15.975) is greater than the table value (2.58) at 0.01, level of significance. So, it is concluded that there does exist significant difference in the Goal Orientation of Higher Secondary School Students based on Medium of Instruction.

Hence, the null hypothesis is rejected.

The Mean Scores show that English Medium Students have higher Goal Orientation.

INFLUENCE OF TYPE OF MANAGEMENT ON GOAL ORIENTATION

Hypothesis-11

There is no significant difference among Higher Secondary School Students' Goal Orientation based on Type of Management.

TABLE.4.11: ANNOVA - Showing Significant Difference in Goal Orientation among Higher Secondary School Students in Relation to Type of Management

Variable	T/M	Sum of squares	Df	Mean Square	F	L.S
Goal Orientation	Between groups	14370.590	2	7185.295	476.650	0.01
	Within groups	9753.250	647	15.075		
	Total	**24123.840**	**649**			

INFERENCE

It is inferred from the above table that the Type of Management has a significant influence on Goal Orientation at **0.01**level.

Hence, the null hypothesis is rejected.

To find out the level of significant difference further analysis is done and represented in the following table

TABLE.4.11: (A) Showing Mean, S.D and t value of Goal Orientation among Higher Secondary School Students based on Type of Management

Variable	Type of management	Number of cases	Mean	S.D	C.R value	L.S
Goal Orientation	Private	260	23.80	4.996	26.451	0.01
	Government	130	11.70	2.108		
	Private	260	23.80	4.996	2.031	0.01
	Govt.Aided	260	23.05	3.238		
	Government	130	11.70	2.108	36.283	0.01
	Govt.Aided	260	23.05	3.238		

The above table shows that there is significant difference in Goal Orientation between Private and Government School Students, Private and Government Aided School Students and Government and Government Aided Students at (0.01) level.

INFLUENCE OF TYPE OF FAMILY ON GOAL ORIENTATION

Hypothesis-12

There is no significant difference among Higher Secondary School Students' Goal Orientation based on Type of Family.

TABLE.4.12: Mean, S.D and t Value of Goal Orientation Classified based on Type of Family

Variable	Type of Family	N	Mean	S.D	t, value	L.S
Goal Orientation	Nuclear	442	21.65	6.605	3.486	0.01
	Joint	208	19.88	4.633		

From the above table, it is observed that the obtained Critical Ratio Value (3.486) is greater than the table value (2.58) at 0.01, level of significance. So, it is concluded that there does exist significant difference in the Goal Orientation of Higher Secondary School Students based on Type of Family.

Hence, the null hypothesis is rejected.

The Mean Scores show that students who belong to Nuclear Family have Higher Goal Orientation.

INFLUENCE OF FAMILY MONTHLY INCOME ON GOAL ORIENTATION

Hypothesis-13

There is no significant difference among Higher Secondary School Students' Goal Orientation based on Family Monthly Income.

TABLE.4.13: Mean, S.D and t value of Goal Orientation Classified based on Mmonthly Iincome

Variable	Family Monthly Income	N	Mean	S.D	t, value	L.S
Goal Orientation	Below 15.000	156	12.92	3.558	29.131	0.01
	Above 15.000	494	23.66	4.148		

From the above table, it is observed that the obtained Critical Ratio Value (29.131) is greater than the table value (2.58) at 0.01, level of significance. So, it is concluded that there does exist significant difference in the Goal Orientation of Higher Secondary School Students based on Family Monthly Income.

Hence, the null hypothesis is rejected.

The Mean Scores reveal that Students' Parents who earn more than Rs.15.000, per month have higher Goal Orientation.

INFLUENCE OF GENDER ON TEMPERAMENT AND ITS DIMENSIONS

Hypothesis-14

There is no significant difference among Higher Secondary School Students' Temperament and its dimensions based on Gender.

TABLE.4.14: Mean, S.D and C.R value of Temperament and its Dimensions Classified based on Gender

Variable	Gender	N	Mean	S.D	C.R value	LS
Effectiveness	Boys	325	16.04	3.566	3.561	0.01
	Girls	325	15.08	3.303		
Cooperativeness	Boys	325	15.84	3.443	0.161	NS
	Girls	325	15.80	2.847		
Interpersonal Sensitivity	Boys	325	15.08	3.434	1.516	NS
	Girls	325	14.72	2.558		
Self-criticism	Boys	325	15.32	3.558	1.157	NS
	Girls	325	15.00	3.492		
Self-focused	Boys	325	16.04	2.724	5.703	0.01
	Girls	325	14.72	3.161		
Social avoidance	Boys	325	15.92	2.745	3.138	0.01
	Girls	325	15.24	2.780		
Irritability	Boys	325	15.20	3.328	2.227	0.05
	Girls	325	14.60	3.538		
Personal reserve	Boys	325	15.36	2.873	2.143	0.01
	Girls	325	14.88	2.837		
Perfectionism	Boys	325	15.36	2.759	0.367	NS
	Girls	325	15.28	2.797		
Anxious worrying	Boys	325	15.20	3.650	1.189	NS
	Girls	325	15.52	3.194		
Temperament (Total)	Boys	325	153.20	27.029	1.457	NS
	Girls	325	150.12	26.878		

From the above table, it is observed in the dimensions Effectiveness, Self-focused, Social Avoidance, Personal Reserve of Temperament, it is found that there is a significant difference at 0.01 level. And in the dimension Irritability of Temperament, it is found that there is a significant difference at 0.05 level. Whereas in the dimensions Cooperativeness, Interpersonal Sensitivity, self-Criticism, Social Avoidance, Perfectionism and Anxious Worrying of Temperament, it is found that there is no significant difference between Boys and Girls.

It is observed in the overall Temperament that the obtained C.R value 1.457 is lesser than the table value (1.96) at 0.05 level of significance. **Hence, the null hypothesis is accepted**.

In the dimensions Effectiveness, Self-focused, Social Avoidance, Personal Reserve and Irritability of Temperament the Mean Scores reveal that Boys have Higher Temperament.

INFLUENCE OF MEDIUM OF INSTRUCTIONS ON TEMPERAMENTT AND ITS DIMENSIONS

Hypothesis-15

There is no significant difference among Higher Secondary School Students' Temperament and its dimensions based on medium of instructions.

TABLE.4.15: Mean, S.D and C.R value of Temperament and its Dimensions Classified based on Medium of Instructions

Variable	Medium	N	Mean	S.D	C.R value	L/S
Effectiveness	Tamil	195	13.00	4.513	14.067	0.01
	English	455	16.66	2.113		
Cooperativeness	Tamil	195	13.53	3.958	13.727	0.01
	English	455	16.80	2.083		
Interpersonal Sensitivity	Tamil	195	12.87	3.603	12.458	0.01
	English	455	15.77	2.246		
Self-criticism	Tamil	195	12.87	4.345	11.990	0.01
	English	455	16.14	2.545		
Self-focused	Tamil	195	13.60	3.583	10.650	0.01
	English	455	16.14	2.371		
Social avoidance	Tamil	195	14.07	3.180	9.713	0.01
	English	455	16.23	2.309		
Irritability	Tamil	195	13.47	3.889	7.212	0.01
	English	455	15.51	3.040		
Personal reserve	Tamil	195	13.53	2.994	9.919	0.01
	English	455	15.80	2.519		
Perfectionism	Tamil	195	13.87	3.210	9.293	0.01
	English	455	15.94	2.307		
Anxious worrying	Tamil	195	13.73	4.370	8.320	0.01
	English	455	16.06	2.653		
Temperament (Total)	Tamil	195	134.53	34.215	11.643	0.01
	English	455	159.00	18.976		

INFERENCE

From the above table, it is observed in the dimensions Effectiveness, Cooperativeness, Interpersonal Sensitivity, Self-Criticism, Self-Focused, Social Avoidance, Irritability, Personal Reserve, Perfectionism and Anxious Worrying of Temperament, it is found that there is a significant difference at **0.01** level.

It is observed in the overall Temperament that the obtained C.R value **11.643** is greater than the table value **(2.58)** at **0.01,** level of significance.

In the dimensions Effectiveness, Cooperativeness, Interpersonal Sensitivity, Self-Criticism, Self-Focused, Social Avoidance, Irritability, Personal Reserve, Perfectionism and Anxious Worrying of Temperament the mean scores reveal that English Medium Higher Secondary School students have higher Temperament.

INFLUENCE OF TYPE OF MANAGEMENTT ON TEMPERAMENTT AND ITS DIMENSION

Hypothesis-16

There is no significant difference among Higher Secondary School Students' Temperament and its dimensions based on type of school management

TABLE.4.16: Annova- Showing Significant Difference in Temperament and its Dimensions among Higher Secondary School Students in Relation to Type of Management

Variable	T/M	Sum of squares	Df	Mean square	F	L/S
EFF	Between Groups	4899.310	2	2449.655	545.614	0.01
	Within Groups	2904.850	647	4.490		
	Total	7804.160	649			
CO	Between Groups	3640.390	2	1820.195	416.792	0.01
	Within Groups	2825.550	647	4.367		
	Total	6465.940	649			
IPS	Between Groups	3072.550	2	1536.275	344.178	0.01
	Within Groups	2887.950	647	4.464		
	Total	5960.500	649			
SC	Between Groups	3833.310	2	1916.655	292.743	0.01
	Within Groups	4236.050	647	6.547		
	Total	8069.360	649			
SF	Between Groups	2972.190	2	1486.095	325.608	0.012
	Within Groups	2952.950	647	4.564		
	Total	5925.140	649			

SA	Between Groups	1997.190	2	998.595	213.714	0.01
	Within Groups	3023.150	647	4.673		
	Total	5020.340	649			
IRR	Between Groups	3355.950	2	1677.975	249.773	0.01
	Within Groups	4346.550	647	6.718		
	Total	7702.500	649			
PR	Between Groups	2460.640	2	1230.320	278.328	0.01
	Within Groups	2860.000	647	4.420		
	Total	5320.640	649			
PER	Between Groups	1950.390	2	975.195	206.663	0.01
	Within Groups	3053.050	647	4.719		
	Total	5003.440	649			
AW	Between Groups	3396.510	2	1698.255	259.068	0.01
	Within Groups	4241.250	647	6.555		
	Total	7637.760	649			
SI (Total)	Between Groups	266412.510	2	133206.255	418.588	0.01
	Within Groups	205893.350	647	318.228		
	Total	472305.860	649			

INFERENCE

It is inferred from the above table that the Type of Management has a significant influence on the dimensions Effectiveness, Cooperativeness, Interpersonal Sensitivity, Self-Criticism, Self-Focused, Social Avoidance, Irritability, Personal Reserve, Perfectionism and Anxious Worrying of Temperament.

Hence, the null hypothesis rejected.

To find out the level of significant difference further analysis is done and represented in the following table.

TABLE.4.16: (A) Showing mean, S.D and t value of Effectiveness Dimension of Temperament among Higher Secondary School Students based on Type of Management

Variable	Type of Management	Number of Cases	Mean	S.D	C.R value	L.S
Effectiveness	Private	260	17.25	1.950	33.962	0.01
	Government	130	10.10	1.980		
	Private	260	17.25	1.950	3.444	0.01
	Govt.Aided	260	16.60	2.337		
	Government	130	10.10	1.980	27.202	0.01
	Govt.Aided	260	16.60	2.337		

The above table shows that there is significant difference in the dimension Effectiveness of Temperament between Private and Government School Students, Private and Government Aided School Students and Government and Government Aided Students at (0.01) level. Private School Students have higher Effectiveness dimension of Temperament than Government and Government Aided School Students.

TABLE.4.16 (B): Showing Mean, S.D and t value for Cooperativeness Dimension of Temperament among Higher Secondary School Students based on Type of Management

Variable	Type of Management	Number of Cases	Mean	S.D	C.R value	L.S
Cooperativeness	Private	260	17.55	1.749	29.915	0.01
	Government	130	11.20	2.367		
	Private	260	17.55	1.749	6.508	0.01
	Govt.Aided	260	16.40	2.249		
	Government	130	11.20	2.367	21.147	0.01
	Govt.Aided	260	16.40	2.249		

The above table shows that there is significant difference in the dimension Cooperativeness of Temperament between Private and Government School Students, Private and Government Aided School Students and Government and Government Aided School Students at (0.01) level. The dimension Cooperativeness of Temperament is higher in Private school students than Government and Government Aided School Students.

TABLE.4.16 (C): Showing mean, S.D and t value for Dimension Interpersonal Sensitivity of Temperament among Higher Secondary School Students based on Type of Management

Variable	Type of Management	Number of Cases	Mean	S.D	C.R value	L.S
Interpersonal sensitivity	Private	260	16.95	2.065	24.155	0.01
	Government	130	11.00	2.694		
	Private	260	16.95	2.065	12.628	0.01
	Govt.Aided	260	14.80	1.809		
	Government	130	11.00	2.694	15.500	0.01
	Govt.Aided	260	14.80	1.809		

The above table shows that there is significant difference in the dimension Interpersonal Sensitivity of Temperament between Private and Government School Students, Private and Government Aided School Students and Government and Government Aided School Students at (0.01) level. The dimension Interpersonal Sensitivity of Temperament is higher in Private School Students than Government and Government Aided School Students.

TABLE.4.16 (D): Showing mean, S.D and t value for Self-criticism Dimension of Temperament among Higher Secondary School Students based on Type of Management

Variable	Type of Management	Number of Cases	Mean	S.D	C.R value	L.S
Self-criticism	Private	260	17.35	2.060	23.758	0.01
	Government	130	10.70	3.450		
	Private	260	17.35	2.060	10.736	0.01
	Govt.Aided	260	15.20	2.487		
	Government	130	10.70	3.450	14.733	0.01
	Govt.Aided	260	15.20	2.487		

The above table shows that there is significant difference in the dimension self –criticism of Temperament between Private and Government School Students, Private and Government Aided School Students and Government and Government Aided School Students at **(0.01)** level. The dimension Self-criticism of Temperament is higher in Private School Students than Government and Government Aided School Students.

TABLE.4.16 (E): Showing Mean, S.D and t value for self-focused dimension of Temperament among Higher Secondary School Students based on Type of Management

Variable	Type of management	Number of cases	Mean	S.D	C.R value	L.S
Self-focused	Private	260	17.25	1.703	30.663	0.01
	Government	130	11.40	1.915		
	Private	260	17.25	1.703	9.119	0.01
	Govt.Aided	260	15.50	2.584		
	Government	130	11.40	1.915	16.021	0.01
	Govt.Aided	260	15.50	2.584		

The above table shows that there is significant difference in the dimension Self –focused of Temperament between Private and Government School Students, Private and Government Aided School Students and Government and Government Aided School Students at (0.01) level. The dimension Self-focused of Temperament is higher in Private School Students than Government and Government Aided School Students.

TABLE.4.16 (F): Showing Mean, S.D and t value for Dimension Social Avoidance of Temperament among Higher Secondary School Students based on Type of Management

Variable	Type of Management	Number of Cases	Mean	S.D	C.R value	L.S
Social Avoidance	Private	260	17.20	1.943	22.512	0.01
	Government	130	12.40	2.067		
	Private	260	17.20	1.943	8.612	0.01
	Govt.Aided	260	15.55	2.402		
	Government	130	12.40	2.067	12.772	0.01
	Govt.Aided	260	15.55	2.402		

The above table shows that there is significant difference in the dimension Social Avoidance of Temperament between Private and Government School Students, Private and Government Aided School Students and Government and Government Aided School Students at (0.01) level. The dimension Social Avoidance of Temperament is higher in Private School Students than Government and Government Aided School Students.

TABLE.4.16 (G): Showing mean, S.D and t value for Irritability Dimension of Temperament among Higher Secondary School Students based on Type of Management

Variable	Type of management	Number of cases	Mean	S.D	C.R value	L.S
Irritability	Private	260	17.30	1.956	27.024	0.01
	Government	130	11.20	2.367		
	Private	260	17.30	1.956	12.717	0.01
	Govt.Aided	260	14.35	3.189		
	Government	130	11.20	2.367	9.971	0.01
	Govt.Aided	260	14.35	3.189		

The above table shows that there is significant difference in the dimension Irritability of Temperament between Private and Government School Students, Private and Government Aided School Students and Government and Government Aided School Students at (0.01) level. The dimension Irritability of Temperament is higher in Private School Students than Government and Government Aided School Students.

TABLE.4.16: (H) Showing Mean, S.D and t value for Personal Reserve Dimension of Temperament among Higher Secondary School Students based on Type of Management

Variable	Type of Management	Number of Cases	Mean	S.D	C.R value	L.S
Personal Reserve	Private	260	17.20	1.753	24.640	0.01
	Government	130	12.00	2.333		
	Private	260	17.20	1.753	14.524	0.01
	Govt.Aided	260	14.60	2.294		
	Government	130	12.00	2.333	10.493	0.01
	Govt.Aided	260	14.60	2.294		

The above table shows that there is significant difference in the dimension Personal Reserve of Temperament between Private and Government School Students, Private and Government Aided School Students and Government and Government Aided School Students at (0.01) level. The dimension Personal Reserve of Temperament is higher in Private School Students than Government and Government Aided School Students.

TABLE.4.16 (I): Showing Mean, S.D and t value for Perfectionism Dimension of Temperament among Higher Secondary School Students based on Type of Management

Variable	Type of Management	Number of Cases	Mean	S.D	C.R value	L.S
Perfectionism	Private	260	17.15	1.593	20.202	0.01
	Government	130	12.50	2.952		
	Private	260	17.15	1.593	13.295	0.01
	Govt.Aided	260	14.90	2.216		
	Government	130	12.50	2.952	8.991	0.01
	Govt.Aided	260	14.90	2.216		

The above table shows that there is significant difference in the dimension Perfectionism of Temperament between Private and Government School Students, Private and Government Aided School Students and Government and Government Aided School Students at (0.01) level. The dimension Perfectionism of Temperament is higher in Private School Students than Government and Government Aided School Students.

TABLE.4.16 (J): Showing mean, S.D and t value for Anxious Worrying Dimension of Temperament among Higher Secondary School Students based on Type of Management

Variable	Type of Management	Number of Cases	Mean	S.D	C.R value	L.S
Anxious Worrying	Private	260	17.55	1.860	24.742	0.01
	Government	130	11.30	3.112		
	Private	260	17.55	1.860	11.149	0.01
	Govt.Aided	260	15.20	2.844		
	Government	130	11.30	3.112	12.366	0.01
	Govt.Aided	260	15.20	2.844		

The above table shows that there is significant difference in the dimension Anxious Worrying of Temperament between Private and Government school Students, Private and Government aided School Students and Government and Government Aided School Students at (0.01) level. The dimension Anxious Worrying of Temperament is higher in Private School Students than Government and Government Aided School Students.

TABLE.4.16 (K): Showing Mean, S.D and t value for Temperament among Higher Secondary School Students based on Type of Management

Variable	Type of Management	Number of Cases	Mean	S.D	C.R value	L.S
Temperament (Total)	Private	260	169.15	14.889	30.700	0.01
	Government	130	113.80	20.056		
	Private	260	169.15	14.899	10.613	0.01
	Govt.Aided	260	153.10	19.311		
	Government	130	113.80	20.056	18.703	0.01
	Govt.Aided	260	153.10	19.311		

The above table shows that there is significant difference in Temperament between Private and Government School Students, Private and Government Aided School Students and Government and Government Aided School Students at (**0.01**) level. The Mean Scores reveal that Private School Students have higher Temperament than Government and Government Aided School Students.

INFLUENCE OF TYPE OF MANAGEMENTT ON TEMPERAMENTT AND ITS DIMENSION

Hypothesis-17

There is no significant difference among Higher Secondary School Students' Temperament and its dimensions based on Type of Family.

TABLE.4.17: Mean, S.D and C.R value of Temperament and its Dimensions classified based on Type of Family

Variable	Type of Family	N	Mean	S.D	C.R value	LS
Effectiveness	Nuclear	442	15.38	3.714	1.908	NS
	Joint	208	15.94	2.846		
Cooperativeness	Nuclear	442	15.79	3.458	0.305	NS
	Joint	208	15.88	2.400		
Interpersonal Sensitivity	Nuclear	442	15.03	3.369	1.589	NS
	Joint	208	14.63	2.123		
Self-criticism	Nuclear	442	15.09	3.819	0.756	NS
	Joint	208	15.31	2.807		
Self-focused	Nuclear	442	15.06	3.156	3.996	0.01
	Joint	208	16.06	2.592		
Social avoidance	Nuclear	442	15.47	2.986	1.463	NS
	Joint	208	15.81	2.275		
Irritability	Nuclear	442	14.94	3.706	0.444	NS
	Joint	208	14.81	2.818		
Personal reserve	Nuclear	442	15.21	3.098	1.115	NS
	Joint	208	14.94	2.282		
Perfectionism	Nuclear	442	15.38	2.984	0.834	NS
	Joint	208	15.19	2.275		
Anxious worrying	Nuclear	442	15.38	3.714	0.242	NS
	Joint	208	15.31	2.739		
Temperament (Total)	Nuclear	442	150.62	29.566	1.437	NS
	Joint	208	153.83	20.300		

INFERENCE

From the above table, it is observed in the dimension Self-focused of Temperament, it is found that there is a significant difference at 0.01 level. Whereas in the dimensions Effectiveness, Cooperativeness, Interpersonal Sensitivity, Self-Criticism, Social Avoidance, Irritability, Personal Reserve, Perfectionism and Anxious Worrying of Temperament, it is found that there is no significant difference between Nuclear and Joint Family of Higher Secondary School Students.

It is observed in the overall Temperament that the obtained C.R value 1.437 is lesser than the table value (1.96) at 0.05, level of significance. **Hence, the null hypothesis is accepted.**

In the dimensions Self-focused of Temperament the Mean Scores reveal that Joint Family of Higher Secondary School Students has higher Temperament.

INFLUENCE OF FAMILY MONTHLY INCOME ON TEMPERAMENTT AND ITS DIMENSIONS

Hypothesis-18

There is no significant difference among Higher Secondary School Students' Temperament and its dimensions based on Family Monthly Income.

TABLE.4.18: Mean, S.D and C.R value of Temperament and its Dimensions Classified based on Family Monthly Income

Variable	Income	N	Mean	S.D	C.R value	LS
Effectiveness	B-15.000	156	11.00	2.717	27.967	0.01
	A-15.000	494	17.00	2.203		
Cooperativeness	B-15.000	156	11.83	2.585	25.688	0.01
	A-15.000	494	17.08	2.097		
Interpersonal Sensitivity	B-15.000	156	11.83	3.115	17.618	0.01
	A-15.000	494	15.87	2.264		
Self-criticism	B-15.000	156	11.50	3.629	18.301	0.01
	A-15.000	494	16.32	2.579		
Self-focused	B-15.000	156	12.17	2.486	18.997	0.01
	A-15.000	494	16.39	2.404		
Social avoidance	B-15.000	156	12.83	2.122	17.001	0.01
	A-15.000	494	16.45	2.372		
Irritability	B-15.000	156	11.50	2.574	16.985	0.01
	A-15.000	494	15.97	2.954		
Personal reserve	B-15.000	156	12.50	2.406	15.278	0.01
	A-15.000	494	15.95	2.473		
Perfectionism	B-15.000	156	12.83	2.803	14.841	0.01
	A-15.000	494	16.11	2.259		
Anxious worrying	B-15.000	156	12.00	3.251	16.800	0.01
	A-15.000	494	16.42	2.733		
Temperament (Total)	B-15.000	156	120.00	23.114	22.364	0.01
	A-15.000	494	161.66	19.306		

INFERENCE

From the above table, it is observed in the Dimensions Effectiveness, Cooperativeness, Interpersonal Sensitivity, Self-Criticism, Self-Focused, Social Avoidance, Irritability, Personal Reserve, Perfectionism and Anxious Worrying of Temperament, that there exist significant difference at **0.01** level.

It is observed in the overall Temperament that the obtained C.R value **(22.364)** is greater than the table value **(2.58)** at **0.01,** level of significance. **Hence, the null hypothesis is rejected.**

In the dimensions of Effectiveness, Cooperativeness, Interpersonal Sensitivity, Self-Criticism, Self-Focused, Social Avoidance, Irritability, Personal Reserve, Perfectionism and Anxious Worrying of Temperament the Mean Scores reveal that the higher Secondary School Students Family whose Income is above Rs.15.000 are having higher Temperament.

CORRELATION BETWEEN HIGHER SECONDARY SCHOOL STUDENTS' SPIRITUAL INTELLIGENCE AND GOAL ORIENTATION

The score related to the correlation between Higher Secondary School Students

Spiritual Intelligence and Goal Orientation is calculated and the details are tabulated in the following table.

TABLE.4.19: Showing the Correlation between Spiritual Intelligence and Goal Orientation among Higher Secondary School Students

Variables	N	R value	L.S
Spiritual Intelligence And Goal Orientation	650	0.903	0.01

INFERENCE

From the above table, it is clearly observed that the R value **(0.903)** is higher than the table value **(0.115)** at **0.01,** level of significance. So, there is significant correlation between Higher Secondary School Students' Spiritual Intelligence and Goal Orientation. **Hence the null hypothesis is rejected.**

CORRELATION BETWEEN HIGHER SECONDARY SCHOOLSTUDENTS' SPIRITUAL INTELLIGENCE AND TEMPERAMENT

The score related to the correlation between Higher Secondary School Students' Spiritual Intelligence and Goal Orientation is calculated and the details are tabulated in the following table.

TABLE.4.20: Showing the Correlation between Higher Secondary School Students' Spiritual Intelligence and Temperament

Variables	N	R value	L.S
Spiritual Intelligence And Temperament	650	0.827	0.01

INFERENCE

From the above table, it is clearly observed that the R value (**0.827**) is higher than the table value (**0.115)** at **0.01,** level of significance. So, there is significant correlation between Higher Secondary School Students' Spiritual Intelligence and Temperament. **Hence, the null hypothesis rejected.**

CORRELATION BETWEEN HIGHER SECONDARY SCHOOLSTUDENTS' GOAL ORIENTATION AND TEMPERAMENT

The score related to the correlation between Higher Secondary School Students' Goal Orientation and Temperament is calculated and the details are tabulated in the following table.

TABLE. 4.21: Showing the Correlation between Higher Secondary School Students' Goal Orientation and Temperament

Variables	N	R value	L.S
Goal Orientation And Temperament	650	0.769	0.01

INFERENCE

From the above table, it is observed clearly that the R value (**0.769**) is higher than the table value (**0.115**) at **0.01,** level of significance. So, there is significant Correlation between Higher Secondary School Students' Goal Orientation and Temperament. **Hence, the null hypothesis is rejected.**

CONCLUSION

Using the datum, each and every hypotheses were carefully analyzed and tested. The result of hypotheses some are accepted and the other are rejected. The findings, summary, suggestions, implications, discussions and conclusion of the research is clearly seen in the following chapter.

❐

5

Summary, Findings, Discussion, Implications, Suggestions and Conclusion

This chapter discusses main findings of the study, discussion of results, delimitations and conclusions of the present study. It furthermore, discusses educational implications and recommendations for future research.

STATEMENT OF THE PROBLEM

The spiritual intelligence in relation to Goal Orientation and temperament among higher secondary students

OBJECTIVES OF THE STUDY

Every research must have some objectives to achieve. The present study aimed at achieving the following objectives:

1. To find out the level of Spiritual Intelligence along with its dimensions among Higher Secondary School Students.
2. To find out the level of Goal Orientation among Higher Secondary School Students.

3. To find out the level of Temperament along with its dimensions among Higher Secondary School Students
4. To find whether there is any significant difference among Higher Secondary School Students' Critical Existential Thinking, Conscious State Expansion, Personal Meaning Production and Transcendental Awareness Dimensions of Spiritual Intelligence based on Gender, Medium of Instruction, Type of Management, Type of Family and Family Monthly Income.
5. To find whether there is any significant difference among Higher Secondary School Students' Goal Orientation based on Gender, Medium of Instruction, Type of Management, Type of Family and Family Monthly Income.
6. To find whether there is any significant difference among Higher Secondary School Students' Effectiveness, Cooperativeness, Interpersonal Sensitivity, Self-Criticism, Self-focused, Social Avoidance, Irritability, Personal Reserve, Perfectionism, Anxious Worrying dimensions of Temperament based on Gender, Medium of Instruction, Type of Management, Type of Family and Family Monthly Income
7. To find whether there is any significant correlation among the variables of the study, namely Spiritual Intelligence, Goal Orientation and Temperament of Higher Secondary School Students.

HYPOTHESES OF THE STUDY

1. The levels of Spiritual Intelligence along with its dimensions among Higher Secondary School Students are moderate in nature.
2. The level of Goal Orientation among Higher Secondary School Students is moderate in nature.
3. The levels of Temperament along with its dimensions among Higher Secondary School Students are moderate in nature.
4. There is no significant difference among Higher Secondary School Students' Spiritual Intelligence and its dimensions (Critical Existential Thinking, Personal Meaning Production, Transcendental Awareness and Conscious State Expansion) based on Gender, Medium of Instruction, Type of Management, Type of Family, and Family Monthly Income.
5. There is no significant difference among Higher Secondary School Students' Goal Orientation based on Gender, Medium of Instruction, Type of Management, Type of Family and Family Monthly Income.
6. There is no significant difference among Higher Secondary School Students' Temperament and its dimensions (Effectiveness, Cooperativeness, Interpersonal sensitivity, Self-criticism,Self-focused,

Social avoidance, Irritability, Personal reserve, Perfectionism and anxious worrying) based on their Gender, Medium of Instruction, Type of Management, Type of Family and Family Monthly Income.

7. There is no significant correlation between Spiritual Intelligence and Temperament among Higher Secondary School Students.
8. There is no significant correlation between Spiritual Intelligence and Temperament among Higher Secondary School Students.
9. There is no significant correlation between Goal Orientation and temperament among higher secondary school students.

SAMPLE OF THE STUDY

Data was collected from the higher secondary school students, adopting stratified random sampling method. Total sample size was 650. Study is done only in Chennai educational district.

TOOLS AND TECHNIQUES USED

To verify the hypotheses formulated in the study, the following tools have been used.

1. Spiritual Intelligence questionnaire constructed by D. King in the year 2008.
2. Goal Orientation inventory was constructed by Dr. Thomas ollikunnal in the 2010.
3. Temperament scale was constructed by Dr. Mathew kallikatt in the year 2014.

COLLECTION OF DATA

Each of the printed copies of answer sheet consisted of a personal data sheet. Spiritual intelligence scale, Goal Orientation scale and temperament inventory scale were distributed to the higher secondary school students and the data were collected personally by the investigator.

ANALYSIS OF DATA

After the data was collected and classified, it was subject to statistical tests of significance for testing the hypothesis formulated by the investigator.
The methods of analysis used were,

- Percentile analysis
- Differential analysis
- Critical ratio
- ANOVA
- Correlation analysis

MAJOR FINDINGS OF SPIRITUAL INTELLIGENCE IN RELATION TO GOAL ORIENTATION AND TEMPERAMENT

It is evident that gender influences the spiritual intelligence. In the dimension critical existential thinking, boys have higher spiritual intelligence (mean score 20.08) than girls (18.92). In the dimension personal meaning production boys and girls do not differ in their spiritual intelligence. Boys have higher transcendental awareness (20.36) than girls (12.96). Boys possess higher conscious state of expansion 13.24 than girls 12.48. In overall spiritual intelligence boys mean score is 66.68 girls mean score is 63.40, so it is found to be boys have greater spiritual intelligence.

TABLE 5.1: Clearly Shows the mean Scores of Spiritual Intelligence and its Dimensions based on Medium of Instruction. It is Found that English Medium School Students have Higher Spiritual Intelligence.

Variable	CET	PMP	TA	CSE	SI
Tamil	15.53	9.27	15.67	10.27	50.73
English	21.20	14.57	21.43	13.97	71.17

Private higher secondary school students have higher spiritual intelligence and its dimensions than government and government aided higher secondary school students.

It was found that Nuclear families have greater spiritual intelligence than joint family in the dimensions critical existential thinking and transcendental awareness. But in the dimensions personal meaning production and conscious state of expansion of spiritual intelligence both nuclear and joint family of higher secondary school students do not have difference. In overall mean scores it is found that nuclear and joint family school students do not differ in their spiritual intelligence.

TABLE.5.2

Variable	CET	PMP	TA	CSE	SI
Nuclear	19.79	13.00	20.09	12.82	65.71
Joint	18.88	12.94	18.88	12.94	63.63

It was found that higher secondary school students' parents, whose monthly income is above Rs.15.000, have higher spiritual intelligence.

TABLE.5.3

Variable	CET	PMP	TA	CSE	SI
Below Rs. 15.000	12.75	7.33	12.92	8.33	41.33
Above Rs15.000	21.63	14.76	21.84	14.29	72.53

Girls and boys do not differ in their Goal Orientation (boys mean score -21.16 and girls mean score-21.00.)

There is a difference in the medium of instruction of higher secondary school students. It was found that English medium higher secondary school students have higher Goal Orientation.

Private higher secondary school students have higher Goal Orientation than the government and government higher secondary school students.

There is significant difference among higher secondary school students' Goal Orientation based on type of family. It is found that students who belong to nuclear family have more Goal Orientation than their counterparts.

There is significant difference among higher secondary school students' Goal Orientation based on family monthly income. It is found that parents of students whose monthly salary is above. Rs. 15.000, have higher Goal Orientation than their counterparts.

There is no significant difference among higher secondary school students' temperament and its dimensions based on gender.

English medium higher secondary school students have higher temperament than the Tamil medium higher secondary school students.

Private higher secondary school students have higher temperament and its dimensions than the government and government higher secondary school students.

There is no difference between nuclear and joint family of higher secondary school students.

There is significant difference among higher secondary school students' parents monthly income whose parents' monthly income is higher than the Rs.15.000 have higher temperament.

DISCUSSIONS ON SPIRITUAL INTELLIGENCE

In the research conducted, it has been concluded that boys have higher spiritual intelligence than girls in higher secondary level. It is mainly owing to the better worldly exposure that boys get more than that of their counterparts in our society. Boys come out to the open world earlier than girls, and have a chance to build rapport with people from all walks of life. Another reason that the findings point out to is that the boys are brought up to be independent, which leads to free thinking and having divergent ideas. They think before they act, and are well aware of their surrounding whom they confront and so on. Such is not in the case of girls, that their rearing is largely overshadowed by others, especially the family, friends and the social environment.

The research states that the students of private schools have better spiritual intelligence than that of the government-aided and the government schools, comparatively less and least respectively. Private managements make the students feel they belong to the learning ambience, and their future is of their main concern. The way the private schools mould the students also answers why they command better spiritual intelligence than any other segment. They teach them how to carry themselves as individuals, how to behave with the fellow-individuals, and how to create an environment of coexistence. In the government-aided schools, the stress on students' spiritual health is comparatively less. They are only to a less degree told about the purpose of their existence and importance of coexistence, which is higher in case of private schools. Looking at the government schools, it is ever so poor as it is the hub of negligence.

The research concludes that the medium of instruction also decides the rate of spiritual intelligence in higher secondary school students. It states that the students belonging to English medium of instruction have high spiritual intelligence against the students of Tamil medium of instruction. It is because of the role that English teachers play in the lives of the students; they not only teach, but also speak beyond the syllabus. The study also affirms that English medium students study English books which are soul-searching and probing in nature. Besides, the way they teach their subjects also stands in stark contrast to the Tamil medium students' way of learning, that new methodologies, innovative techniques make the former think differently and finally arrive at the point from where they start thinking of their existence and so on.

Type of family, be it nuclear or joint, does not show any difference in the amount of spiritual intelligence among the higher secondary school students, puts the study. It is because students hailing from both familial environments have parents and the other members in the family to shape them. In addition, the time that a higher secondary school student spends with his/her family is relatively low, that there is hardly any room left for them to be influenced. Furthermore, as it is the time of upper adolescence, the group that a student forms with his/her friends commands more influence than that of a closed setting like their family.

The research settles that students whose parent's monthly income is above Rs. 15,000 possess higher spiritual intelligence than that of the parent's whose income is any lesser than that. It also reasons out that for the former, there is no economic strain from the family. Since family economy is stable and satisfactory, the home is free from any domestic problems. This directly affects the student whose parents are perfectly in peace with each other and therefore he/she can think about the individual self and the world around. Had he/she been confronted with economic problems, it would have led to mental distress which in turn would have affected their life.

DISCUSSIONS ON GOAL ORIENTATION

The research in its findings affirms that there is no difference in terms of Goal Orientation on the bases of gender. Starting from kindergarten, every child is asked the following question: "What is your ambition?" such is the awareness that the students receive to set goals in their lives. Gone are those days when only boys were allowed to enter into professions and girls pushed to backyard. In contrast, now, every boy and girl has his/her own dreams of becoming so and so. Further, both of them are given freedom to choose profession of their own choice. There is nothing that hinders a girl to aim and become so; from her family, friends, to school, everyone has begun placing her at the equal footing with that of a boy.

The research directs to a conclusion that students of private schools have better Goal Orientation that that of either government-aided or government schools. Since private schools have got dedicated teachers, the motivation and the inputs that the students receive there is far high comparing to that of the government-aided and government school students. Private school students are given awareness as which path will lead to where, and its consequences. As the teachers in the private schools have better know-how in the field of career guidance, they steer the students in apt path than that of the rest two. As the very aim of private schools itself is towards some goal, they better equip their students in Goal Orientation. Such is not in the case of government-aided schools, that they are only partially concerned about the students' future. Worst is in the case of government schools, that not only really cares about the students and his/her future.

As per the findings of the research, students in English medium schools have better Goal Orientation than that of those in Tamil medium. It is because of the confidence of English medium school students that they have in their job competency. They are confident since the present-day job market hunts for those who know English and therefore they are assured of success. Such being the case, whatever little activity they may partake, they do it with a goal-oriented mind which leads to their success in later bigger activities. On the other hand, students in Tamil medium schools comparatively less confident of themselves and therefore are unsure of facing the future. There is hardly anyone to nudge them to set goals and push them to work towards achieving it.

The research states that the students hailing from nuclear family have an edge over those from joint family when it comes to Goal Orientation. It is because of the attention the former gets from the nuclear family makes them to be much goal-oriented. As there would be too many in a joint family, the attention gets diverted and a student is not in much of a focus. As there are only parents in the nuclear family, they encourage their child to set goals and monitor the progress. They also speak with the student's teachers and discuss it. Though there are many in a joint family, it does not mean that the amount of encouragement that a student gets is high. It only leads to a feeling of being left in a crowd and feeling aloof. In a nuclear family, the student feels that he belongs to the family and therefore leads to better goal-orientation.

Goal-orientation, states the research, is high for the students whose parents receive a monthly income of above Rs. 15,000 comparing to that of the students whose parents receive below than that. It is because the amount of attention that the former gets is comparatively high than that of the latter. In the second case, as the parents would be obsessed with the thought of earning, they would not have enough time to spend with their child and get to know in what direction he/she is headed. Their prime focus would be to somehow to scrape through money from somewhere. As the financial needs are met with in the first case, they spend time with their child and get to know his/her world better than the latter. In the first case, the student is aware of his/her family's limitations and thus sets out to carve a better future for him/her and his/her family. This is the reason why the students whose parents earn above Rs. 15,000 a month have better goal-orientation.

DISCUSSIONS ON TEMPERAMENT

The research states that boys have better temperament than that of the girls. It is mainly due to the exposure that the former gets to the outside world makes the difference. As Boys know how to be by themselves and with others, it makes them adapt to any condition. The more they involve in activities, the greater is the chance of their being stuck in problems. Such being the case, they experience how to solve a problem too. This also decides their emotional level and their response to the external environment. The more closed the girls are, the fewer is the chance of their involvement in problem-solving. They are often than not left alone to themselves and the relationship with the outside world is relatively less.

In terms of temperament, students from private schools have better than that of those both at government-aided and government schools, shows the research. Private schools take care to create a rich learning environment which decides the students' temperament. Private schools arrange for activities outside the curriculum that best shapes the personality of the students. Vibrant sporting activities, debates, educational tours, camps, visit to museums and exhibitions are a few examples of how action-packed is the ambience in private schools. This is the exposure that the students in private schools get opposed to that of the remaining two. Students from Government-aided schools have less temperament comparing to that of those in private schools. Least is the position of government schools in this head. It is because the students those who join here would be mostly from slums and poor families, the awareness of temperament is very less comparing to that of those in private schools.

The research has concluded that the students studying in English medium schools have better temperament than that of those in Tamil medium schools. In the English medium schools, the pupils are taught how to build a personality, how to behave in a group, how to confront problems and how to be efficient in whatever they do. This is not so in Tamil medium schools. Furthermore, in English medium schools, students are taught of various skills that make up to form a personality. English medium schools provide learning beyond classroom, which in turn shapes their temperament. Learning ambience in English medium schools is not monotonous and instead, it is vibrant.

According to the findings of the research, the type of a student's family also has a bearing in his/her temperament. Students hailing from nuclear families have better temperament than that of those from joint families. It is because the former is better monitored at home than the latter. The students from nuclear families have clear head and new ideas opposed to that of the students from joint families who have complicated thinking. As the latter hails from the conventional family setting, it greatly affects their temperament.

The research states that the students who parents earn above Rs. 15,000 a month have better temperament than that of those whose parents earn less than that. It is because there would be no frustration in the former that shapes their temperament better. The economy of the family does not reach the child, so he/she is worried about himself/herself and not about the family. This makes them face the challenges and shape their personality better than the students who are temperamentally shaky.

EDUCATIONAL IMPLICATIONS OF THE STUDY ON SPIRITUAL INTELLIGENCEIN RELATION TO GOAL-ORIENTATION AND TEMPERAMENT

Spiritual intelligence of an adolescent affects his/her goal-orientation and temperament. Spiritual intelligence is the need of the hour as adolescence is characterized by emotional swings. Teacher should inculcate in a student an awareness of self and how to balance oneself with others. An adolescent should be infused with the need to coexist with others who differ in ideas, opinions, religion, caste, language etc.

Spiritual intelligence enables a student to have higher goal-orientation. Spiritually intelligent student will not be worried about the future as he/she would know what to aim for. Taking decisions becomes relatively easier when a student is spiritually intelligent. Spiritually intelligent student is able to prioritize his/her needs according to their level of importance. A student finds many ways to achieve a goal when he/she is spiritually intelligent. Spiritual intelligent student has clear thoughts and does not complicate things. Teachers must orient a student towards goals as they would cut down on unnecessary diversions. Teachers should give constant motivation in the aspect of setting goals and never dropping out until they are realised. Teachers should boost up in such a way that a student would develop interest from within.

When a student is spiritually intelligent, he/she would settle nothing less than perfection. Teachers should not let the complacency creep in the mind of a student who has realised his/her goals. Instead, he/she should be motivated to aim higher and higher. Teachers should treat everyone equal so that a student also develops the habit of treating people of differences equally. When a student is spiritually intelligent, he/she will be able to check his/her temper. Accepting differences and adapting to the changes are possible only when an adolescent is spiritually intelligent. Spiritually intelligent student will not get irritable if he/she is confronted by persons he/she dislikes.

Spiritual intelligence develops the quality of tolerance in a student. A student should be told of the consequences of losing temper as it would break relationships. Spiritual intelligence fosters broadmindedness which in turn makes a student cooperative. Teacher should inculcate in an adolescent that values are much more important than any other worldly things. Extra-curricular activities like yoga, meditation, sports and games must be given importance as they would enhance a student's emotional balance.

Spiritual intelligence shapes a student's maturity. Spiritual intelligent student makes himself/herself agreeable to everyone so that he/she could be encouraged to exert his/her influence in others too. Value education should find a place in the curriculum. The curriculum framer should frame the curriculum as value-based. The government should conduct seminars and workshops on regular basis to spread awareness among teachers to inculcate values in the students. Parents of the students should also be given necessary counselling as how to handle their adolescent children.

Spiritual intelligence can be improved with training. A number of techniques, strategies, and practices have been identified as beneficial for development and enhancement SI. There are essentially seven ways to raise or develop spiritual intelligence. They include:

- Think about your goals, desires and wants to bring your life into perspective and balance and identify your values.
- Access his/her inner processes and use visualization to see his goals, desires and wants fulfilled; and experience the emotion connected with this fulfilment.

- Integrate one's personal and universal vision and recognize his connectedness to others, to nature, to the world and to the universe.
- Take responsibility for one's goals, desires and wants.
- Develop a sense of community by letting more people into one's life.
- Focus on love and compassion.
- When chance knocks at one's door, let it in and take advantage of Coincidences.

Suggestions for Further Research

Though the present investigation has been carried out with due care and thought regarding various aspects of the research work, it may continue to have some shortcomings which have been realized during the conduction of the research .Being conscious of the short comings some suggestions are being made here for further investigations in this area:

- The sample was restricted to Chennai city only. The sample for the data Collection could be outside Chennai city so that a comparative study between the different schools / departments of two or more universities may be carried out.
- The sample of the study can include different streams i.e. arts, science
- Commerce and social science. Different departments should be included in the sample also.
- Other variables suggested for further research are emotional intelligence, cultural Intelligence aptitude, creativity, Study habits etc. on Spiritual Intelligence. Moreover, these variables could give some interesting findings.
- Larger sample provide better results, but the present research work is confined to only 650 senior secondary students. Thus it cannot claim for its comprehensiveness. Future researches may be conducted on even larger. The result may provide greater insight for students and researchers.

CONCLUSION

This chapter discussesthe main findings of the study, discussion of results, limitations and conclusions of the present study. It furthermore, discusses the educational implications and recommendations for future research.

❐

6

The Problem and its Perspectives

Excellence in education in every country aims at developing a learning society and creates its own system of education. To attain and promote its unique socio cultural identity and also to meet the challenges of the times, the systems of education needs to be revitalized. The traditional rural society is moving towards modernization and globalization. The steady movement towards mechanization, industrialization and urbanization with the growth of mass society is catching up fast even in the field of education. Telecommunication links have speeded up the business activities. The political and news services with the country and with the rest of the world. Transport from place has become more rapid and frequent people are not only better informed but more mobile. This newly emerging society has to evolve a new educational system to meet the future challenges.

MEANING OF SOCIAL INTELLIGENCE

Various individuals are using learned social skills to improve thequality of the life and relationships. Most of human psychological problems were associated with the society. The psychological problem like depression, fear, confusion, anger created by the lack of positive human emotions is critical to the happiness of the individual in the society. SoSocial Intelligence is created to bring the skills in to the world of human interaction and relations.

According to E.L. Thorndike(1920) the term intelligence refer the person ability to understand and manage the people and also engage in adopt in social interaction. It also refers the individuals' fund of knowledge about the social word (Kihlstrom 1987).

Social Intelligence is the ability to understand and manage boys and girls and act wisely with human relations similarly, Moss and Hunt (1927) defined social intelligence as the "ability to get along with others" Vernon (1933) defined social intelligence as the person's "ability to get along with people in general ability to handle".Social intelligence is highly combined with the personal and social competenceand this is vital for healthy and productive life. Such intelligence is comprised of social competence, social awareness, and social skills. But these are very difficult measuring and various related researchers are proving that there is a direct relationship exist between these skills and the productivity of life (Emmerling 1999)

DEFINITION OF SOCIAL INTELLIGENCE

According to **HOWARD GARDENER (1983)**"Social Intelligence is the capacityto know oneself and to know others is on inalienable a part of the human condition as it is the capacity to know objects of sounds and it deserves to be investigated not less than these other less charged forms."

NEEDS OF SOCIAL INTELLIGENCE

Although anyone benefit from social intelligent training it has especially successful with the following groups.

- People in high stress jobs
- Single (or) divorced men and women who could like to find a bid a healthy relationship.
- Workers in regular contact with the public
- Married partners who should like to action higher levels of intimacy with one another.
- Organizational trainers and instructors.

Social Intelligence and instructors based not theoretical. The material is brought to life by skilled trainers who demonstrate problems and state solutions that work in the every duty world.

DEVELOPMENT OF SOCIAL INTELLIGENCE

George Herbert mead described, "The whole nature of intelligent as social to its very core". In this respect, he was a fore runner of social construction, which, when applied to psychotherapy, focuses the therapeutic process on the client's. Meaning-making processing the context of relationships. Furthermore, mead perceived the primary aspect of human intelligent to be the capacity of the individual to "put himself in the place of another. The implications of this for both individual and family psychotherapy and in particular its relevance to the practices of empathy and dialogue are explored. A case of couple therapy is used to illustrate the specific applications of the theoretical concepts discussed.

It is generally recognized that the specific social expressions of intelligent depend upon the given individuals ability to take the roles of, or "put himself in the place of" the others individuals implicated with him in given social situations and upon his consequent sensitivity to their attitudes towards himself and towards one another, these specifically social expressions of intelligence, of course acquire unique significance in terms of our view that the whole nature of intelligence is social to its very core, that this putting of one's self in the place of theirs, this taking by one's self of their roles or attitudes, is not expressions of intelligence of intelligent behavior, but is the very essence of its character.

FACTORS OF SOCIAL INTELLIGENCE

- Patience, cooperativeness, confidence level, sensitivity, recognition of social environment, tactfulness, sense of humor, memory.
- Patience-calm endurance under stressful situations.
- Cooperativeness-ability to interest with other in a pleasant way to be able to view matters from all angles.
- Confidence level-firm trust in one's self and one's chances.
- Sensitivity-to be actually aware of and responsive.
- Recognition of social environment – ability to perceive the nature and atmosphere of the existing situations.
- Tactfulness – decline perception of the right thing to say or do.
- Sense of humor – capacity to feel and cause amusement to be able to see the lighter side of life.
- Memory – ability to remember all relevant issues; names and faces of people.

MEANING OF SELF-ESTEEM

Self-esteem is a type of self-concept. It is a positive or negative orientation towards oneself, on overall evaluation of one's worth or value. People are motivated to heave high self-esteem and indicates positive regard, not egotism, self-esteem is onlyone component of self-concept, it is the totally of the individuals thoughts and feelings with reference to himself as an objective. Besides self-esteem, self-efficacy or mastery and self-identities are important parts of self-concept.

DEFINITIONS ON SELF-ESTEEM

SYMONDS (1951) defined "Self-Esteem has different kind's self-evaluation and self – affection from different forms of positive experience affiliation and task success."

WHITE (1954) defined "Self-Esteem is a kind of self – respect having its basis in the person's sense of competence and efficiency."

COHEN (1959) defines Self-Esteem as "The degree of correspondence between an individual his ideals and actual concept of himself".

ROSENBERG (1965) defined "Self-Esteem as the evaluation which the individual makes and customarily maintain with regards to himself and expressed at an attitude of approval."

COOPERMITH (1967) "Self-Esteem is a personal judgment of worthiness that is exposed in the attitudes that individuals holds towards themselves".

PSYCHOLOGICAL BACKGROUND OF SELF-ESTEEM

The social scientists of recent years are very much interested in the concept of self-esteem the personal evaluation of oneself and the feelings of worth is in association with one's self concept which forms the most important aspects of Self-esteem.

According to **Maslow (1968)** human needs are placed into five groups – coding to the order of the hierarchy.

- Physiological needs
- Safety or security needs
- Need for love and belonging
- Esteem needs
- Self-actualization needs

Maslow puts fourth self-esteem at the fourth stage and everyone should go through three previous stages to attain self-esteem. It is also a pre-condition for self-actualization esteem needs are divided into two categories.

- Self-Esteem, self-respect, self-regard & self –education
- Reputation, status, social success and fame

Maslow believed that sufficient gratification of the Self-esteem needs reduce their dominating force in a person's life, thus enabling him to move in the direction of self-actualization.

Cooper Smith(1967) has noted that failure to gratify the need for self-respect or reputation from others can produce personality disturbance in the individual.

DEVELOPMENT OF SELF-ESTEEM

Several processes have been identified as important as important to the development of self-esteem reflected appraisals, social comparisons, and self-attributions. Within sociology, reflected appraisals are the most important process because of its emphasis within symbolic interaction theory. The reflected appraisals process states that everyone see ourselves and evaluate ourselves as others see think and evaluate themselves. It is important to emphasize that the reflected appraisals process operates through our perceptions of the appraisals of others.

Another process important to the development of self-esteem is social comparison. This is the process in which individuals assess their own abilities and virtues by comparing them to those of others. According to **Leon Festinger's (1954)** theory, as well as well as much of the contemporary theory and research on social comparison, the main function of this process is reality-testing. Individuals tend to compare themselves with others who are doing slightly better than themselves (upward social comparison) as a means of gathering information about a specific task.

Daryl Bern's (1972)self-perception theory proposes that individuals acquire knowledge about themselves in the same way they acquire knowledge about others: by observing behavior and making inferences about internal dispositions and states (e.g., motives, attitudes, self-esteem) from these observations.

Although all three of these processes are important to the development and maintenance of self-esteem, at any one time one time one may be more relevant to self-esteem than the others. Also, it is evident that the self does not passively respond to processes in the interests of protecting self-esteem is both a product of social forces and an agent in its own development (**Gecas 2001**).

PHASES OF SELF-ESTEEM

The three phases of self-esteem are identifying phase, nurturance phase, maintenance phase in which the adolescent tries to achieve his identify by achieving Self-esteem as they are interrelated.

Identity Phases

An individual with low Self-esteem needs to discover his own identity. Because of distorted perception, such persons rarely have a clearly understandingwho they really are usually such person do not see their whole self but focus onsmall aspects of self. It is necessary therefore that they develop their own identify.This identity serves as a foundation for the further development of self-esteem.

Nurturance Phase

In the nurturance phase, the individual was taught how to nurture the newly found identitywith its strengths and weaknesses. The nurturance phase is importantas it helps individuals understand owe to broaden their perspective on their own self-esteem and enrich it. This phase focus in the development of a social support system that includes bearing how to filter feedback from the environment and managing self-talk.

Maintenance Phase

The final phase of enhancing self-esteem is maintenance. After one is aware of who self is what his strength and weakness are and strategies for nurturing self, thereis a need to learn how to maintain adequate self-esteem at various phases in one's life, this process of change is more rapid than at other times. It is essential to maintain self-esteem as it is necessary to maintain interpersonal relationship if it is to grow and flourish. Activities in this phase focus on goal setting, rise taking and personnel forecasting.

Self – esteem is a type of self-concept. It is a positive and negative orientation towards oneself, an overall evaluation of one's worth or value. People are motivatedto have high self-esteem and indicates positive self-regard, not egotism. Self –Esteemis only one component of self-concept. It is the totality of the individual's thoughtsand feelings with reference to himself as an object. Besides self-esteem, self-efficacyor mastery and self-identities are important parts of self-concept.

TYPES OF SELF-ESTEEM

High Self-Esteem

The person loves themselves and accepts who they are. Those who possess high self-esteem can be described to have high self-confidence being happy, wholesomeness, a feeling of being in control, thinking positively, being in charge, assertive behavior, having self-respect, vitality, being at ease, being dynamic, dignified, feeling balanced, successful, charismatic personality and have a sense of Security.

Low Self-Esteem

A person who does not love onself, doesn't accept oneselfand doesn't value one's own qualities. Aperson with low self-esteempossesses, the following characteristic features likes lacking self-confidence, being unhappy, a feeling of not belonging, being out of control, thinking negatively, disempowered, being depressed, not energetic, feeling shameful and shakes, weak personality and feeling of insecurity and failure

Inflated Self-Esteem

The person loves oneself more than others and exaggerates thequalities present in him.

SELF-ESTEEM IN ADOLESCENTS

Self-esteem maintains the overall well-being. Self-esteem involves in its dimension the evaluation process of self. Global Self-esteem has been described by **Rosenberg (1979)** as the overall negative or positive attitude towards self. The sources for self-esteem development rests primarily in reflected appraisals and social comparisons. Young people compare their competences to those of their peers to discern their level of worth.

Cooper Smith (1967), Estein (1973) and Hotter (1983) all delimited four dimensions the evaluate process of self-esteem. Competence or success in meeting achievement demands. Social acceptance, or attention worthiness and positive reinforcement received from others. Control of feelings of internal responsibility for outcomes. Virtue or adherence to moral and ethical standards. Rosenberg emphasized the importance of the reflected self and of social comparison in determining self-esteem, as well as the importance of doing well in the areas valued by the individual.

According to **Erickson (1968)** the four tasks of adolescents are attainment of independence, establishment of a sexual role and orientation, self-control of aggressive and oppositional impulses, achievement of self-identity.

STATEMENT OF THE PROBLEM

The problem is entitled as ***"A study on Social Intelligence and Self-Esteem among higher secondary students"***.

OPERATIONAL DEFINITIONS

Social Intelligence

Socialization involves the complementary process of individualization and along with social development the child also develops "social intelligence". A positive or favorable self-esteem towards one's life, help in developing Social Intelligence.

By this investigator means the total score obtained in the Social Intelligence Scale prepared and standardized by Dr .N.K. Chanda (1990)

Self-Esteem

Self-Esteem is the individual's way of looking at one's abilities and personality it also signifies his way of thinking, feeling and behaving. Self-Esteem is one of the aspects of personality pattern, and it governs the individual's characteristic reaction to people and situations.

By this the investigator means the cores obtained from the Self-Esteem Inventory M.S.Prasad, G.P.Thakar (1989).

OBJECTIVES OF THE STUDY

The following objectives are set in the present study.

1. To find out the level of Social Intelligence of higher secondary students.
2. To find out the level of Self-Esteem among higher secondary students.
3. To find out whether there is any significant difference between mean scores of Social Intelligence of higher secondary students based on Gender.
4. To find out whether there is any significant difference between mean scores of Social Intelligence of higher secondary students based on Type of Management.
5. To find out whether there is any significant difference between mean scores of Social Intelligence of higher secondary students based on Type of Family.
6. To find out whether there is any significant difference between mean scores of Social Intelligence of higher secondary students based on Father's Qualification.
7. To find out whether there is any significant difference between the mean scores of Social Intelligence of higher secondary students based on Mother's Qualification
8. To find out whether there is any significant difference between the mean scores of Social Intelligence of higher secondary students based on Birth Order.
9. To find out whether there is any significant difference between the mean scores of Social Intelligence of higher secondary students based on Family Monthly Income.
10. To find out whether there is any significant difference between the mean scores of Self-Esteem among higher secondary students Based on Gender.
11. To find out whether there is any significant difference between the mean scores of Self-Esteem among higherSecondary students based on Type of Management.
12. To find out whether there is any significant difference between the mean scores of Self-Esteem among higher secondary students based on Type of Family.
13. To find out whether there is any significant difference between the mean scores of Self-Esteem among higher secondary students based on Father's Qualification.
14. To find out whether there is any significant difference between the mean scores of Self-Esteem among higher secondary students based on Mother's Qualification.

15. To find out whether there is any significant difference between the mean scores of Self-Esteem among higher secondary students based on Birth Order.
16. To find out whether there is any significant difference between the mean scores of Self-Esteem among higher secondary students based on Family Monthly Income.
17. To find out whether there is any significant correlation among the variables of Social Intelligence and Self-Esteem among higher secondary students.

NEED FOR THE STUDY

Self-esteem is an important dimension in the field of education. A student's ambition can be fulfilled only through his test performance in school. It's the foundation stage of higher secondary school students to get prepared for entry into higher secondary for a better performance in academics. Adolescence is highly critical period of any student's life to cope with academic performance. Self-esteem of each and every student are to be identified and molded specially.

The investigator would like to see at the higher secondary level whether the two variables, lead suitable self-esteem and leadership behavior are interrelated and whether there is mutual inter dependence the finding may lead suitable measures to improve the self-esteem of higher secondary students.

DELIMITATIONS OF THE STUDY

The present study had the following delimitations

- In this study the investigator focuses only on Social Intelligence and Self-Esteem though there are other factors that may also influence the student behavior.
- Data collection is restricted to Chennai District only
- The present study is restricted exclusively to Plus One higher secondary students.
- The investigator has selected only three types of school viz., government, government aided and private.
- The sample is restricted to 300 only.

CONCLUSION

The problem of the present study has been discussed briefly in this chapter, bringing out the need for the study, objectives of the study. Operational definition of the terms used in this study. A review of the related literature available has been scanned to the theoretical perspective in this study to throw light for formulation appropriate hypotheses which could be tested. A detailed discussion of the related literature bearing on the problem in hand follows in the next chapter. ❐

7

Review of Related Literature

One of the most important preliminary steps in the research process is doing a thorough review of the literature on the topic identified for study. A review of literature is the process of locating, obtaining, reading and evaluating the research literature in a area of interest. Perhaps the most important reasons for conducting a literature review are to avoid needless duplication of effort. Literature review applies to the design phase of a research. Review of related literature keeps up to date on current empirical or theoretical controversies in research area, controversies gives direction to specific research hypothesis and design.

ROLE OF RELATED LITERATURE IN A RESEARCH PROJECT

The search for related literature serves important functions.

- Knowledge of related research enables investigates to define the frontiers of their fields.
- Review of literature is for the purpose of findings a link between one's study and the accumulated knowledge in one's study and the accumulated knowledge in one's field of interest.

STUDIES RELATED TO SOCIAL INTELLIGENCE

Studies in Abroad

Cantor &Kihistrom (1987, 1989)viewed social intelligence as a traitor group of traits, on which individuals can be compared and ranked on a dimension from low to high. Rather, the social intelligence view of personality begins with the assumption that it is mediated by cognitive processes of perception, memory, reasoning and problem solving, rather than being mediated be innate reflexes, conditioned responses, evolved genetic problems. Accordingly, the social intelligence video construes individual differences in social behavior — the public manifestations of personality to be the product of individual differences in the knowledge which individuals bring to bear on their social interactions. Difference in social knowledge cause differences in social behavior but it does not make sense to construct measures of social IQ. The important variable is not how much social intelligence the person has, but rather what social intelligence he or she possesses.

Sullivan et al. (1965) conducted a normative study in which 306 high school students received 23 different social intelligence tests representing the six hypothesized factors, along with 24 measures of 12 nonsocial ability factors. A principal factor analysis with orthogonal rotation yielded 22 factors, including the 12 nonsocial reference factors and six factors clearly interpretable as cognition of behavior. In general, the six behavioral factors were not contaminated by non-social semantic and spatial abilities. Thus, 0' Sullivan et al. apparently succeeded in measuring expressly social abilities which were essentially independent of abstract cognitive ability. However, echoing earlier findings with the GWSIT, later studies found substantial correlations between IQ and scores on the individual Guilford subtests, as well as various composite social intelligence scores (Riggio. Messamer&Throkmorton, 1991; Stanley, walker & Foley, 1971). Still Stanley et al conceded that the correlations obtained were not strong enough to warrant the conclusion (e.g., Wechsler, 1958) that social intelligence is nothing more than general intelligence applied in the social domain.

Gabrielsen, Eric (1992) examined of the role of self-monitoring in choice of college major. A self-monitor is an individual who adopts a social orientation so that he/she can manage self-presentation. Self-monitors are likely to modify their academic choices to fit social situations or others expectations. Data were collected using a four — part questionnaire that explored background, a self-monitoring scale, a personal freedom versus social conformity scale and a friendship scale. Result indicated that self-monitoring played a role in selection of college majors. However, data also indicated that the direct influence of close friends was not what most persuaded self-monitors with regard to choice of major.

BoulonDiaz, Frances (1992) studied school achievement with the following variables intelligence, social class, early motor and language development, preschool experience, gender and composition of household. The subjects were 65 children of 9 to 1 years, in grades four to six, in Puerto. Rican Public schools. They were selected from the sample of 2,200 children used for adapting the Wechsler Intelligence Scale for children revised for the Puerto Rican population. The Wisc — R Puerto Rico was used to measure IQ.

Mathias, Jane. L. (1992) conducted a study on Social intelligence with 75 adolescents with mental retardation. Factor analysis measures of conceptual intelligence, adaptive behaviour and Social intelligence yielded a practice — interpersonal competence construct. The second study however failed to establish the criterion validity of this construct.

Nettelbeck Ted (1992) defined Social intelligence, with a total of 125 adolescents with mental retardation, found high to very high integrator reliability coefficients; moderate to very high internal reliabilities; and moderate to high test — retest reliabilities.

Burke, Robin (1993) described "Story Producer for Interactive Learning" (SPIEL) a multimedia retrieval system for educational stories, mid its integration into an architecture called "Guided Social Simulation" (CUSS), for teaching complex social skills such as management, diplomacy or selling.

Davenport, Elizabeth (1993) assessed Social intelligence from the perspectives of information management, information policy and information economics, - reviews tools and techniques associated with Social intelligence, including networks, hypermedia and connectionism and consider education and training for Social intelligence.

Michael, William. B. (1993) determined how accurately each of several hypothesized combinations of first — order and higher - order factors reflecting creativity in the social intelligence of 192 high school students described the co variation in selected sub matrix from the total correlation matrix originally analyzed.

Laosa Luis, M. (1995) studied that there is a resurgence of scientific and public interest and controversy centering on four interrelated themes: intelligence testing, racial, ethnic and Socio-economic differences in measures IQ, genetic and environmental influences on abilities and the role of scientific research in social policy. Given the polarization of views, dispassionate discussion is needed to help inform the ongoing debate.

Kay Bjorkqrist et al. (2000) studied empathy and social intelligence are strongly correlated, it is, for both logical and consequential reasons, important to regard them as different concepts. Social intelligence is required for all types of conflict behavior, prosaically as well as antisocial, but the presence of empathy acts as a mitigateof aggression. When empathy is partial out, correlations between social intelligence and all types of aggression increases, while correlations between social intelligence and peaceful conflict resolution decreases. Social intelligence is related differently to various forms of aggressive behavior: more strongly to indirect than to verbal aggression and weakest to physical aggression, which is in accordance with the developmental theory of aggressive style. More sophisticated forms of aggression require more social intelligence.

Lee .J. E et al. (2000) conducted the present study of social and academic intelligence with the purpose (1) to replicated previous research on social intelligence that shows social intelligence to be multidimensional in nature and distinguishable from academic intelligence, (2) to extend prior research by assessing whether the crystallized or fluid distinction discussed in the academic intelligence literature was applicable to the domain of social intelligence and (3) to explore whether a hierarchical model of social and academic intelligence was consistent with the data. One hundred and sixty-nine university students completed verbal, pictorial and self-report measures of four constructs: Social knowledge (hypothesized to reflect crystallized social intelligence), social inference (hypothesized to reflect fluid social intelligence), crystallized academic and fluid academic intelligences. In addition, other-report measures were collected for these constructs in this multi trait-multi method study. Confirmatory factor analysis replicated previous research, documenting that the four trait constructs showed convergent and discriminate validities. Similar analyses also extended prior research by showing that the crystallized or fluid distinction might be applicable in the social intelligence domain (although the evidence was stronger for crystallized social intelligence the fluid social-intelligence) and that a hierarchical model fits the data well.

EleniAndreou. (2006) studied the relations among social preference, perceived popularity, social-intelligence and two types of aggressive behavior were studied. Peer-estimation techniques were used to measure all major variables. Altogether, 403 Greek School children from fourth-through sixth grade class rooms participated in the study. Both overt and relational aggression was negatively associated with social preference for girls; overt aggression was positively associated with perceived popularity for boys. Relational aggression was positively associated with perceived popularity for both boys and girls and social information processing only for girls. In addition, as was hypothesized, relational aggression was predicted by cognitive aspects of social intelligence whereas overt aggression by lack of social skills. Overt aggression was found to be a unique significant negative predictor of perceived popularity whereas relational aggression a positive predictor. Implications for intervention are discussed.

Susanne weis and Heinz Martin, (2006) studied social-intelligence as a performance construct and thus is based on Thorndike's idea of social-intelligence as a mental ability distinct from abstract and mechanical intelligence (1920). So far, there has been only limited success in identifying a unitary social intelligence construct distinct from academic intelligence. The objects of our study were two fold First we intended to demonstrate the multi dimensionality of social intelligence. We postulated three cognitive ability domains (i.e. social-understanding memory, and knowledge) these domains were operationalized in a multi trait-multi method design applying verbal, pictorial and video based performance measures. Secondly, we intended to demonstrate that social intelligence can be differentiated from academic-intelligence. One hundred and eighteen high school and first year psychology students were tested. Confirmatory factor analysis yielded generally low validity Co-efficient between social and academic intelligence expect for the social memory tests. Still, residual analysis showed unique common variance within the social memory domain. Consequently, the study provided evidence for the structure of the study provided evidence for the structure of the social intelligence performance model according to the postulated design and demonstrated the discriminability of social intelligence from academic intelligence.

STUDIES IN INDIA

Buch, M.B. (1960) for assessed the social intelligent of individuals quantitatively and to study the effect of environmental factors as grades as occupational status of social intelligence. The subjects for the present study of social intelligence were selected on the basis of certain independent findings supported by the content analysis of the available test of social intelligence. The sub tests included here were: judgments in social situations, memory for names and faces, observation of human behaviour, recognition of the mental and faces, observation of human behavior, recognition of the mental state of the speaker, sense of humor and social introduction.

Ray, T. (1972) aimed at developing test in Bengali for the objective measurement of social intelligence. Final form of the test had eighty items distributed on six different area of human behaviour namely: judgments in social situations, memory for names state of the speaker, sense of humor and social introduction.

Giles (2004) conducted a study to find out how celebrities influence they younger generations and is related to their social networks. He studied the relationship between celebrity interests, attachment to parents and peer and emotional autonomy among a sample of 191 adolescents who worship celebrities for entertainment and social reasons had a high attachment to peer. They were group players. They were self-confident. Peer interaction is an important feature of celebrity attachment.

Windle, m., Mason, w.a., et al. (2004) studied the general and specific predictors of behavioural and emotional problems among adolescents. Based on a simple of 1,218 students in the 10th and 11th grades, 14 variables measuring behavioural and emotional problems were modeled as four factors via confirmatory factor analysis. The factors were labeled polydrug use, delinquency, negative affect, and academic orientation. Significant predictors common to the four factors included stressful life events and family social support. Specific predictive relations were indicated for particular temperament attributes and specific problem factors (e.g. high activity level predicted delinquency; behavioural inflexibility predicated negative affect)

Lenin R. (2005) conducted an investigation into peer relationship and social intelligent of teacher trainees, who were studying under university of madras. The sample consists of 293 students from six teacher training colleges in Chennai. It was found that the level of social intelligence and peer relationships of teacher trainees in moderate is nature and there is a significant relation between peer relationship and social intelligence.

Wright Robin, Dewit et al. (2005) studied the methodology and program effects of the secondary schools demonstration project (SSDP) conducted in four Ontario schools. The objective of the study was to evaluate to which a universal program model of three interventions-cooperative learning, classroom management and peer-helping approaches that include tutoring and mediation-can reduce the prevalence of antisocial behaviour. The study employed a two-group matched comparison before-and-after design. It involved the collection of baseline data on all ninth grade students (average age of 14 years) in four schools, and the selection of a subsample for a more detailed follow-up. Of the 13 measures analyzed, the results were statistically significant on four variables student perception of teacher, student sense of belonging, student attachment to school and truancy, suspensions and behaviour problems. The findings of the study are discussed in relation to the methodological issues involved in implementing and evaluating multi-component interventions in secondary schools.

Estell David B. (2009) conducted a study of bullying and victimization in 5th grade classrooms in relation to students' education status and peer group membership. The sample consisted of 484 participants (258 girls, 226 boys), including 369 general education students, 74 academically gifted students, and

41 students with mild disabilities were more likely to be perceived as bullies by both teachers and peers. Teachers also rated students with mild disabilities significantly higher for being bullied by peers. Academically gifted students were rated by teachers as the lowest for both bullying and being bullied. Associating with aggressive or perceived-popular peers increased the likelihood of being perceived as a bully. Social isolates were more likely to be bullied than students who did not associate with perceived popular peers.

Knoester, Matthew (2009) conducted a study on connections among adolescent engagement with reading, peer relationship, and identity development. The author chose and interviewed 10 of his former student, their parents, and the students' current teachers. The case studies illustrate how "independent reading" is a social practice in crucial ways.

Stampoltzis, Aglaia, Polychronopoulos, Stavroula, et al. (2009) made a study exploring the personal and educational experiences of Greek students with dyslexia in higher education. Interviews with 16 students with dyslexia (11 male and five female) were conducted to investigate how they experienced school, peer relations, labeling, family support, university, self-esteem and how they made their future plans. Data were analyzed using thematic analysis. Primary school was remembered by interviewees as a series of unhappy and distressing memories that had a negative effect on their self-esteem. As they grew older, problems were more limited to academic skills, and they developed friendships with peers. The time in which they were diagnosed as dyslexic was important because it opened the way to adaptation. Students with dyslexia experienced a variety of difficulties at university, and employed a number of coping strategies to deal with them. The findings of the present study seem to indicate that the recipe for a favorable outcome appears to be early diagnosis, explanation of the diagnosis to the student, parental support and suitable teaching and help at school and at university. Further research is needed into how to make schools and universities more "dyslexia friendly", and on how the secondary effects of dyslexia can be reduced.

STUDIES RELATED TO SELF-ESTEEM

Foreign Studies on Self-Esteem

Nassari, Gholamreza (1975) studied Self Esteem test anxiety and general anxiety among students of three ethnic groups in grades 9 to 12. This dissertation investigated the levels of self Esteem, general anxiety and test anxiety and their inter-relationships among White, Black and Spanish surnamed students in grades nine to twelve.

Kong, Xuqun (1999) examined both the mediation effects of loneliness and self-esteem for the relationship between social support and life satisfaction.

Three hundred and eighty nine Chinese college students, ranging in age from 17 to 25 (M = 20.39), completed the emotional and social loneliness scale, the self-esteem scale, the satisfaction with life scale and measure of social support. Structural equation modeling showed full mediation effects of loneliness and self-esteem between social support and life satisfaction. The final model also revealed a significant path from social support through loneliness and self-esteem to life satisfaction. Furthermore, a multi-group analysis found that the paths did not differ across sexes. The findings provided the external validity for the full mediation effects of loneliness and self-esteem and valuable evidence for more complicated relations among the variables.

Nicole: Phillips, Clan (2001) examined the impact of positive psychological traits (positive coping, self-efficacy, and self-esteem) on the relationship between seizure severity and life satisfaction among individuals with epilepsy. Hierarchical regression analysis and correlation techniques were used to test a hypothesized tri-mediation model of life satisfaction for individuals with epilepsy. Results indicated that seizure severity and positive human traits, including positive coping, self-efficacy, and self-esteem, were indeed associated with overall life satisfaction. Self-efficacy and self-esteem (but not positive coping) fully mediated the relationship between seizure severity and life satisfaction, lending support for a dual-mediation model. These findings suggest there may be considerable value for rehabilitation psychologists and counselors to develop specialized intervention programs that focus on capitalizing these positive human traits to promote life satisfaction and well-being for clients with epilepsy.

Degges-White, Suzanne (2004) conducted a study of 320 women, ages 21 to 69, explored the relations among relationship status, subjective age, self-esteem, and life satisfaction. Women in married or partnered relationships had higher levels of life satisfaction than did single women. Women in their 30s and 40s had significantly lower levels of life satisfaction than did other age groups.

Kapikiran, Sahin (2004) aimed to measure whether self-esteem and social support are mediators in the relationship between loneliness and life satisfaction. The study includes early teenagers from the 6th, 7th and 8th grades aged between 11 and 15 (M = 13.31, SD = 1.09). The study group consisted of 431 secondary school students from large and medium sized cities in Turkey, of which 196 (44.5%) were girls and 235 (54.5%) were boys. The study examined students' responses to life satisfaction, loneliness, self-esteem and social support scales. Data were separated into parcels of instruments within the framework of structural equation modeling. It was determined that both self-esteem and social support were partial mediators between loneliness and life satisfaction. These results are discussed within the scope of the literature.

Civitci, Asim (2005) studied the effects of global self-esteem on the relationship between life satisfaction domains (family, friends and school) and depression in early adolescents were examined. The participants consisted of 255 students, aged from 11 to 15 years, from three junior high schools in Turkey. Data were collected using the Rosenberg Self-esteem Scale, the Multidimensional Students' Life Satisfaction Scale, and the Children's Depression Inventory. Results indicated that self-esteem moderated the relationship between depression and family satisfaction, but not between depression and friend satisfaction and school satisfaction.

STUDIES IN INDIA

Nisha (1991) examined adolescent alienation in relation to personality values adjustment, self-esteem and academic achievement. The tools used are Bell's adjustment inventory and Rosenberg's self-esteem scale. The major findings were: Adolescents high on alienation differed significantly from those who were low on alienation on the score of all dimensions of personality, value, income, social, emotional and total adjustment and self-esteem. Adolescents of 16 to 17 years high on alienation differed significantly from low on time adjustment values and adjustment.

Phinnely Jean et al. (1992) in their study on acculturation attitudes and self-esteem of high school and college students to survey acculturation among 417 high school and 223 college students from Asian-American, Africa-American. Results suggested positive effects for self-esteem, maintaining identification with one's culture and the mainstream culture.

BloteAnke W (1995) studied student's self-concept in relation to perceived differential teacher and found student and teacher perceptions of differential teacher behavior toward good and not-so-good students. Students and teachers agreed that low-achieving students got more teacher support, but they differed in their views of amounts of praise and criticism.

Craig S (1995) investigated the relationship between family cohesion, family adaptability and student's satisfaction with family and self-esteem among 619 middle school students. Analysis indicates that within the specified model, family satisfaction was the strongest predictor of student self-esteem and that eighth grade student reported significantly lower level of family cohesion and family satisfaction than did sixth grade student.

Katayal (2000) examined children's perception of parental disciplinary practices and its relationship with their self-esteem and dependent proneness. It further assessed children's perception of parental disciplinary practices and its relationship with their self-esteem and dependent proneness. A sample of 100 boys and 100 girls were administered the parental disciplinary practice scale,

Coppersmith self-esteem and the dependence proneness scale This study revealed the children's positive perception was significantly

Donald G.Garder(2004) conducted a study on "self-esteem within the work and organizational context" On numerous research works it has been suggested that an individual's self-esteem, formed around work and organizational experiences, plays a significant role in determine employee's motivation, work related attitudes and behaviors We review more than a decade of research on an organization based conceptualization of self-esteem It is observed that sources of organization structure and signals about worth from the organization.

Lowery, Sarah E. (2005) conducted the study on "Body image, self-esteem and health related behaviours among male and female first year college students". This study examined the relationship among self-esteem, body image and health related behaviors. Data were collected in 23 classrooms. Social-esteem was consistently related to body image dissatisfaction for women. Even when both image. Finally, for men and women, more positive physical fitness/ health-related behaviors were positively related to self-esteem and body image on, as well as success-building role conditions predict organized based self-esteem.

Claudia Garcez (2006) conducted a study on "Job satisfaction and self-esteem". The main objective of this study is to bring the relationship between job satisfaction and self-esteem. These groups of professionals include psychologists, sociologists and professors. The research consistently provides support for the notion that a person who is satisfied with their job has a higher self-esteem than who is not. A person who has a high self-esteem is likely to be more satisfied with their job.

Jon L. Pierce (2006) conducted a study on "Self-Esteem and Self-Efficacy within the organizational climate". The self-concept has emerged as an important component of organizational paradigms. This article reviews the conceptual meanings of self-esteem and self-efficacy, clarifies the relationship between the generalized self-efficacy and explored two outcomes – employees job performance and job related affect organization based self-esteem emerged as the stronger predictor of ratings of performance and employees satisfaction and it appears to act as a mediator in the relationship between generalized self-efficacy and these employee responses. The managerial implications are also discussed in this study.

Peggy Dalgas (2006) conducted a study on "Effects of a self-esteem intervention program on school-age children". The development of a strong sense of self-esteem during childhood is important if children are to withstand the family stresses, social pressures and temptations of deviance encountered at earlier stages of life. Such evidence suggests that higher levels of self-esteem may lead to more success in life and greater motivation for health maintenance behaviours. Thus, providing preventive self-esteem development intervention at an early age is especially important.

Winston J. Hagborg (2006) conducted a study on "Self-esteem and self-perception of adolescents". The Rosenberg self-esteem scale is widely used to measure self-esteem. The sample for this study consisted of 150 adolescents randomly drawn in equal numbers and equated by gender from grades 8 to 12. The conclusion of this study is that self-esteem and that its two identified factors are essentially measuring one rather than two different constructs. Other findings include a gender difference, with females reporting significantly lower RSE scores and modest co relational support for a grade level rise found in the literature.

Ruben G. Rumbaut (2007) conducted a study on "Ethnic identity, self-esteem and segmented assimilation among the children of immigrants". Focusing on the information of ethnic self-identities during adolescence, this article examines the psychological adaptation of children of immigrant Asia. The results show major differences in their patterns of ethnic self-identification both between and within groups from devices national origins.

CONCLUSION

The study of related literature has helped the investigator to have a clear perspective of the problem chosen for the present investigation. Keeping abreast of the work done in this field, the researcher has formulated the hypotheses for the present study. Designing the method of research, description of the variables, sample selection, selection of suitable tools, administration and scoring methods of responses have been undertaken based on the review which is discussed in the succeeding chapter.

❒

8

Research Design and Methodology

In the modern society research has become an important activity for its very progress. Research produces new knowledge which takes the society forward. It enables to find the solutions to the problems and resolve conflicts in the society.

Research has been defined as "A studious inquiry or Examinations; especially critical and exhaustive or experimental having for its aim the discovery of new facts and their correct interpretation, the revision of accepted conclusions, theories or laws in the lights of newly discovered facts or partial applications of new or revised conclusions, theories or laws." (Webster, 1981)

Develop new scientific tools, concepts and theories which would facilitate reliable and valid study of human behavior in decision making. (Aggarvan and Diwan, 1997)

The research process can be viewed as "the overall scheme of scientific activities in which scientific inquiry" (Frankfort- Nachmmias, 1992). Scientific activities satisfy the criteria of logical verification. The knowledge produced thus is provable both through reason experience or observation.

This chapter gives an overall picture of the design of the study, the form of hypotheses to be tested, research tools used for the collection of data, its reliability and validity of the tools, pilot study, nature and collection of the sample, a brief description of the procedure adopted for the data collection, scoring and statistical techniques to be employed for the analysis of data.

VARIABLES SELECTED

The following variables were selected for the study.

Experimental Variables

- Social Intelligence
- Self-Esteem

Personal Variables

- Gender
- Type of Family
- Father's Qualification
- Mother's Qualification
- Birth Order
- Family Monthly Income

School related variable

- Type of Management

HYPOTHESES OF THE STUDY

1. The researcher has formulated the following hypotheses pertaining to the present study.
2. The levels of Social Intelligence among the higher secondary students are moderate in nature.
3. The level of Self-Esteem among higher secondary students is moderate in nature.
4. There is no significant difference between the mean scores of Social Intelligence among higher secondary students based on Gender.
5. There is no significant difference between the mean scores of Social Intelligence among higher secondary students based on Type of Management.
6. There is no significant difference between the mean scores of Social Intelligence among higher secondary students based on Type of Family.
7. There is no significant difference between the mean scores of Social Intelligence among higher secondary students based on Father's Qualification.
8. There is no significant difference between the mean scores of Social Intelligence among higher secondary students based on Mother's Qualification.

9. There is no significant difference between the mean scores of Social Intelligence among higher secondary students based on Birth Order.
10. There is no significant difference between the mean scores of Social Intelligence among higher secondary students based on Family Monthly Income.
11. There is no significant difference between the mean scores of
12. Self-Esteem among higher secondary students based on Gender.
13. There is no significant difference between the mean scores of
14. Self-Esteem among higher secondary students based on Type of Management.
15. There is no significant difference between the mean scores of
16. Self-Esteem among higher secondary students based on Type of Family.
17. There is no significant difference between the mean scores of
18. Self-Esteem among higher secondary students based on Father's Qualification.
19. There is no significant difference between the mean scores of
20. Self-Esteem among higher secondary students based on Mother's Qualification.
21. There is no significant difference between the mean scores of
22. Self-Esteem among higher secondary students based on Birth Order.
23. There is no significant difference between the mean scores of
24. Self-Esteem among higher secondary students based on Family Monthly Income.
25. There is no significant correlation between the Social Intelligence and Self-Esteem among higher secondary students.

METHOD OF STUDY

As the study intends to collect data pertaining to the school social intelligence and self-esteem for the higher secondary students, normative method is employed to describe and interpret what exists at the present scenario. It involves some types of comparison or contrast and attempts to discover relationship between existing non-manipulated variables. The normative study is one of the commonly used approaches in solving the educational problems.

TOOLS USED

To collect the pertinent data for the present investigation, standardized tools have been employed to quantify the variables involved in the study.

1. The investigator has used the following tools for the data collection. They are listed below:
2. Personal data sheet consists of details like Gender, Type of Management, Type of Family, Father's Qualification, Mother's Qualification, Birth Order and Family Monthly Income.

3. Social Intelligence Scale prepared was constructed by Dr.N.K.Chandha(1990)
4. Self-Esteem M.S.Prasad, G.P.Thakar(1989)

SOCIAL INTELLIGENCE SCALE

Description

Social Intelligence Scale (APPENDIX-I) consists of 54 items and 12 pictures of persons constructed by Dr. N. K. Chadha (1990).

Administration

The social intelligence tool is constructed with simple sentences. The following instructions were given to the subjects before administrating the test. "There are some statements regarding the way in which we behave, feel and act. We want your first response. Please try to make your best possible answer honestly and sincerely. Read and understand each question properly and then put your mark on any cell against every statement on the answer sheet by making the sign of cross (X) please do not omit any question. In part I read the following statements carefully and among the three responses given for each of them, pick up the one which seems to you to be the most likely way in which you would respond. You are to choose only one response from a,b and c, and mark a cross (X) on the appropriate cell on the answer sheet. In part II select the word that most accurately describes the mental state of the person making the statement. Cross out (X) the correct answer on the answer sheet. In part III there are some statements regarding the way you behave and act. Each statement has a forced choice response of either 'yes' or 'no' , try and decide whether 'yes' or 'no' represents your usual way of behaviour and acting. If yes, cross out (X) the cell below 'no'. In part IV list of incomplete jokes are given. Against them, there are three choices with which to complete the joke. You are to select and cross out (X) the choice you consider to be the most humorous. In part V list of eminent persons are given."

Scoring Procedure

In the case of the first four dimensions (Patience, cooperativeness, Confidence and sensitivity) scores of 1,2, and 3 were given to three response alternatives. For e.g., in the confidence dimension a score of 3 would indicate a high degree of confidence, a score of 1 a lack of confidence and a score of 2 would reveal moderate confidence. In the other two dimensions (sense of humor and recognition of social environment), one of three alternatives given is the appropriate response. This response when given was allotted of scores of 1. In the case of the 'Tactfulness' dimensions the response were in the form of 'yes' or 'no'. The appropriate response was awarded a score of '1'. The last dimension that of Memory was scored '1' or '0' depending on whether or not the subject's response was 'right' or 'wrong'.

SELF-ESTEEM SCALE

Description

The Self-Esteem Inventory (SEI) consists of relevant statements regarding the self-esteem of students. The inventory consists of 30 and includes statement of self-confidence, self-reliance, and self-control etc., such as that he/she thinks about themselves and what others think about them. This is devised by M.S Prasad and G.P Thakur (1989), psychology department, University of Bihar.

Administration

The Self-Esteem Inventory was administered to the respondents in groups among the regular students. Reading of the instruction by the examiner to the group, however, ensures better conditions for responding to the items of the inventory. The answers were recorded by the respondents on the scale.

There was no time limit for answering the statements, but they were asked to complete it as early as possible. At the end they were asked to check whether they had expressed their opinion about every statement. In this manner, the administration procedure was carried out.

Scoring

Each item was accorded a seven point response score; the intervals of which was labeled as

- Totally correct
- Correct to be a large extent
- Partially correct
- Uncertain
- Partially wrong
- Wrong to a large
- Totally wrong

The successive response intervals subsequently were scored as 7,6,5,4,3,2 and1 where the high score represents high Self-esteem. The answer were checked against the key and points were given for each item and ticked as per the key. The total points obtained gave a measurable of Self-esteem.

TABLE.8.1: Showing Scoring Key of the Statement According to the Nature of Items

Nature of items	Totally correct	Correct to a large extent	Partially correct	Uncertain	Partially wrong	Wrong to a large extent	Totally wrong
Positive 1,3,4,5,7,8,10,11,12,14,16,19,20,22,23,25,29	7	6	5	4	3	2	1
Negative 2,6,9,13,15,17,18,21,24,26,27,28,30	1	2	3	4	5	6	7

SAMPLE DISTRIBUTION

The sample distribution of the sample included in the study has been presented as below.

TABLE.8.2: Showing the Sample Distribution of the Present Study

S.No.	Management of the School	Boys	Girls	Total
1	Government Schools	50	50	100
2	Aided Schools	50	50	100
3	Private Schools	50	50	100
Total		**150**	**150**	**300**

PILOT STUDY

A pilot study was conducted in the month of November 2014 to determine the suitability of the tools used in the present investigation. A random sample of 50 higher secondary students was selected to the study for establish the reliability and validity of the tools.

RELIABILITY AND VALIDITY OF THE TOOLS

SOCIAL INTELLIGENCE

Reliability

Social intelligence scale Test- Retest is used in establishing the reliability of the scale. Karl Pearson's product moment 'r' is worked out for these two sets of scores and it was found to be 0.804 which reliability co-efficient.

Validity

Further index of reliability could also be taken as a measure of validity and this works out to be the square root of the reliability 0.897, which is high valid questionnaire.

SELF-ESTEEM

Reliability

The reliability of a test may be defined as the degree of consistency with which the test measures what it measures a test scores is called reliable, when we have a reason to believe it to be stable and trust worthy.

In order to establish the reliability of the Self-esteem inventory the split half method was used. The reliability of Self-esteem was found to be 0.6020. The reliability of Self-Esteem inventory was considered to be highly reliable.

Validity

Validity means the ability to produce findings that are in agreement with conceptual or theoretical values. If refers to the success of the scale in measuring what it meant to measure. A test is valid, when it measure, truly and accurately the ability or quality one wants to measure. Thus, validity means truthfulness of the test.

The Index of validity which is the square root of reliability was found to be 0.78 and it is found to be highly valid.

Sample

The present study is concerned with higher secondary schools. Hence, the higher secondary students from various Government, Government Aided Schools and Private Schools were taken to constitute the population for the present study. The stratified random sampling technique was adopted in the present study. The size of the sample was 300.

TABLE.8.3: Showing the Sample Distribution of Schools in the Present Study

SL. No.	Name of the school	Type of the management of the schools	Number of students selected		
			Boys	Girls	Total
1.	A G S Nidhi Higher Secondary School	Government	50	50	100
2.	Bishop Corry Anglo Indian Higher Secondary School	Aided	50	50	100
3.	St. Montfort Matriculation Higher Secondary School	Private	50	50	100
	Total	**150**	**150**	**300**	

MAIN STUDY

The investigator conducted and obtained permission from the Principals/ Heads of the selected for data collection in Government schools. The correspondent/Secretary of the Government Aided and Private schools were contacted to get permission to collect data from their schools. The willingness and co-operation of the respective class teachers were also sought.

The data were collected personally by the investigator from the selected 300 pupils in the month of December 2014. Proper instructions were given to the pupils before starting to fill the Questionnaire. Each pupil was provided with a set of tools containing personal data sheet, a school social intelligence and self-esteem questionnaire. Pupils were requested to mark their responses in the space provided in the tools itself. In order to facilitate the clear understanding of the statements in the tools, the investigator read out each statement loudly using simple terms wherever necessary.

After having ascertained that the pupils have responded the particular item. The investigator passed on the next. Students were requested not to omit any of the items. Finally the filled in questionnaire were collected from the students.

STATISTICAL TECHNIQUES USED

Mean

$$\text{Mean (x)} = A + \frac{\sum fd}{\sum f} \times i$$

Where,

A = Assumed mean

f = frequency

d = deviation from the assumed mean

i = Class interval

Standard Deviation

$$\text{Standard Deviation, } SD\ (\sigma) = \sqrt{\frac{\sum fd^2}{N} - \left[\frac{\sum fd}{N}\right]^2} \times i$$

Where,

f = Frequency

d = Deviation from the assumed mean

I = Class interval

N = Total frequency

't' test

To continue the significance of difference between means of various measures test is used: 't' ratio is calculated from the relation.

$$\text{t-ratio} = \frac{M_1 \sim M_2}{\sqrt{\frac{\sigma_1^2}{N_1} + \frac{\sigma_1^2}{N_2}}} = \frac{M_1 \sim M_2}{S \in D}$$

Where,

M_1 M_2= Means of the groups

SED = Standard Error Deviation

'F'-Test

F- ratio = Variance between the group/ Variance within the group Correction term 'C'

$$C = \frac{\sum x_1 + \sum x_2 + \sum x_3}{N}$$

$$BSS = \left(\sum x_1\right)^2 / W_1 + \left(\sum x_2\right)^2 / W_2 + \left(\sum x_3\right)^2 W_3 - C$$

$$TSS = \sum x_1^2 + \sum x_2^2 + \sum x_3^2 - C$$

WSS= TSS - BSS

Where,

x_1, x_2, x_3, are score in different group

C = correction Terms

TSS = Total Sum of Squares

BSS = Between Sum of Squares

WSS = Within Sum of Squares

Co-Efficient of Correlation(r)

$$r = \frac{N \sum x \sum y - \sum x \sum y}{\sqrt{\left(N \sum x^2 - \left(\sum x^2\right)\right)\left(N \sum y^2 - \left(\sum y\right)^2\right.}}$$

x, y – Variables,
N- Total strength.

CONCLUSION

This chapter outlines the statement of the problem, operational definition of key terms, objective of the study, hypotheses design of the present study, the procedure followed and the nature of the population, sample size and sampling techniques. It describes the hypotheses to be tested, the tools used and the methods of administration and scoring, and delimitation of the study. The obtained scores were analyzed using appropriate statistical techniques described in this study on students personal problems, study involvement and academic achievement and present in the next chapter.

❒

9

Analysis and Interpretation of the Data

Analysis of data is an important step in quantitative research

According to **Mouly** (1964) "Research data becomes meaningful in theprocess of being analyzed and interpreted". The key phase of every thesis is the proper analysis and interpretation of the data.

According to **Carter V good, states** "The purpose of interpretation is essentially one of stating what the finding conveys? What is their significance? What is the answer to the original problem?

This chapter presents the results obtained from the analysis of data collected from the students of higher secondary schools based on two variables viz., social intelligence and Self-Esteem. The data has been subjected to

1. Descriptive,
2. Inferential and
3. Correlation statistics

DESCRIPTIVE ANALYSIS

Categories of the sample based on Social Intelligence

Hypothesis-1

The level of Social Intelligence among higher secondary students is moderate in nature

TABLE.9.1: Showing the levels of Social Intelligence among Higher Secondary Students

Variable	Group	Score Range	Frequency	Percentage
Social Intelligence	Low	101 and below	79	26.3
	Moderate	101-130	144	48
	High	131 and above	77	25.7

INFERENCE

From the above table it is known that, more number of students are present in the range Between 101 to 130.

It shows that the level of social intelligence of higher secondary school students is moderate in nature. Hence the **hypothesis 1 is accepted.**

Categories of the sample based on Self-Esteem

Hypothesis-2

The level of Self-Esteem among higher secondary students is moderate in nature.

TABLE.9.2: Showing the levels of Self-Esteem among Higher Secondary Students.

Variable	Group	Score Range	Frequency	Percentage
	Low	27 and below	78	26
Self-Esteem	Moderate	28-36	145	48.3
	High	37 and above	77	25-8

INFERENCE

From the above table it is known that, more number of students are present in the range between 28 to 36.

It shows that the level of Self-Esteem of higher secondary school students is moderate in nature.

Hence the **hypothesis 2 is accepted.**

INFERENTIAL ANALYSIS

INFLUENCE OF GENDER ON SOCIAL INTELLIGENCE

Hypothesis – 3

There is no significant difference between the mean scores of Social Intelligence among higher secondary students Based on Gender

TABLE.9.3: Showing the mean, S.D and C.R value for of Social Intelligence with Based on Gender

Variable	Gender	Number of cases	Mean	S.D	CR	L.S
Social Intelligence	Boys	150	97.98	10.81	0.230	NS
	Girls	150	95.17	10.80		

INFERENCE

From the table, it is clear that the obtained CR value (0.230) is lower than the table value (1.96) at 0.05 level of significance.

It shows thatthere is no significant difference between the mean scores of Social intelligence among higher secondary students with regard to Gender. Hence the **hypothesis 3 is accepted.**

INFLUENCE OF TYPE OF MANAGEMENT ONSOCIAL INTELLIGENCE

Hypothesis – 4

There is no significant difference between the mean scores of Social Intelligence among higher secondary students based on Type of Management.

TABLE.9.4: Showing ANOVA for Social Intelligence of Higher Secondary Students based on Type of Management.

Variable		Sum of Squares	df	Mean Squares	'F' Value	L.S
Social Intelligence	Between Groups	3.387	2	1.69	0.014	N.S
	Within Groups	34781.450	297	117.109		
	Total	34781.450	299			

INFERENCE

From the above table, it is clear that the obtained F value (0.014) is lower than the table value (3.03) at 0.05 levelof significance. Itshows that there is no significant difference between the mean scores of Social intelligence amonghigher secondary studentsbased on Type of Management. Hence the **hypothesis 4is accepted.**

INFLUENCE OF TYPE OF FAMILY ON SOCIAL INTELLIGENCE

Hypothesis – 5

There is no significant difference between the mean scores of Social Intelligence among higher secondary students based on Type of Family.

TABLE.9.5: Showing the Significant Difference between the mean Scores of Social Intelligence with Respect to Type of Family

Variable	Type of Family	Number of Cases	Mean	S.D	C.R Value	L.S
Social Intelligence	Joint	763	97.88	10.81	0.230	N.S
	Nuclear	227	93.53	10.88		

INFERENCE

From the table, it is clear that the obtained CR value (0.230) is lower than the table value (1.96) at 0.05 level of significance.

It shows that there is no significant difference between the mean scores of Social intelligence among higher secondary students with regard to type of family. Hence the **hypothesis 5 is accepted.**

INFLUENCE OF TYPE OF FATHER'S EDUCATIONAL QUALIFICATION ON SOCIAL INTELLIGENCE

Hypothesis – 6

There is no significant difference between the mean scores of Social Intelligence among higher secondary students based on Father's Qualification

TABLE.9.6: Showing ANOVA for Social Intelligence of Higher Secondary Students based on Father's Educational Qualification.

Variable		Sum of Squares	df	Mean Squares	'F' Value	L.S
Social Intelligence	Between Groups	406.149	2	203.074	1.754	N.S
	Within Groups	34378.688	297	115.753		
	Total	**18893.289**	**299**			

INFERENCE

From the table, it is clear that the obtained F value (1.754) is higher than the table value (3.03) at 0.05 level of significance.

It shows that there is no significant difference between the means scores of Social intelligence among higher secondary students. with regard to Father's Educational Qualification. Hence the **hypothesis 6 is accepted.**

INFLUENCE OF MOTHER'S EDUCATIONAL QUALIFICATION ON SOCIAL INTELLIGENCE

Hypothesis – 7

There is no significant difference between the mean scores of Social Intelligence among higher secondary students based on Mother's Qualification

TABLE.9.7: Showing ANOVA for Social Intelligence of Higher Secondary Students based on Mother's Educational Qualification.

Variable		Sum of Squares	df	Mean Squares	'F' Value	L.S
Social Intelligence	Between Groups	682.982	2	341.491	2.974	N.S
	Within Groups	34101.854	297	144.821		
	Total	18893.289	299			

INFERENCE

From the table, it is clear that the obtained F value (2.974) is lower than the table value (3.03) at 0.05 levelof significance.

It shows thatthere is no significant difference between the mean scores of Social intelligence among higher secondary students with regard to Mother's Educational Qualification.

Hence the **hypothesis 7is accepted.**

INFLUENCE OF BIRTH ORDERONSOCIAL INTELLIGENCE

Hypothesis – 8

There is no significant difference between the mean scores of Social Intelligence among higher secondary students based on Birth Order.

TABLE.9.8: Showing ANOVA for Social Intelligence of Higher Secondary Students based on Birth Order.

Variable		Sum of Squares	df	Mean Squares	'F' Value	L.S
Social Intelligence	Between Groups	226.236	2	113.12	0.972	N.S
	Within Groups	34558.601	297	116.36		
	Total	**34784.837**	**299**			

INFERENCE

From the table, it is clear that the obtained F value (0.972) lower than the table value (3.03) at 0.05 level of significance.

Its hows that there is no significant difference between the mean scores of Self-esteem among higher secondary student with regard to birth order.

Hence the **hypothesis 8 is accepted.**

INFLUENCEOF FAMILY MONTHLY INCOMEONSOCIAL INTELLIGENCE

Hypothesis – 9

There is no significant difference between the mean scores of Social Intelligence among higher secondary students based on Family Monthly Income.

TABLE.9.9: Showing ANOVA for Social Intelligence of Higher Secondary Students based on Family Monthly Income.

Variable		Sum of Squares	df	Mean Squares	'F' Value	L.S
Social Intelligence	Between Groups	226.236	2	113.12	0.972	N.S
	Within Groups	34558.601	297	116.36		
	Total	**34784.837**	**299**			

INFERENCE

From the table, it is clear that the obtained F value (0.972) lower than the table value (3.03) at 0.05 level of significance.

Its hows that there is no significant difference between the mean scores of Self-esteem among higher secondary student with regard to family monthly income.

Hence the **hypothesis 9 is accepted.**

INFLUENCE OF GENDER ON SELF-ESTEEM

Hypothesis –10

There is no significant difference between the mean scores of Self-Esteem among higher secondary students based on Gender.

TABLE.9.10: Showing the mean, S.D and C.R value for of Self-Esteem with Respect to Gender

Variable	Gender	Number of cases	Mean	S.D	CR Value	L.S
Self esteem	Boys	150	144.89	19.086	0.128	N.S
	Girls	**150**	145.18	20.476		

INFERENCE

From the table, it is clear that the obtained CR value (0.128) is lower than the table value (1.96) at 0.05 level of significance.

Its hows that there is no significant difference between the mean scores of self-esteem among higher secondary students with regard to Gender.

Hence the **hypothesis 10 is accepted.**

INFLUENCE OF TYPE OF MANAGEMENT ON SELF ESTEEM

Hypothesis – 11

There is no significant difference between the mean scores of Self-Esteem among higher secondary students based on Type of Management

TABLE.9.11: Showing ANOVA for Self-Esteem of higher secondary students based on Type of Management.

Variable		Sum of Squares	df	Mean Squares	'F' Value	L.S
Self- Esteem	Between Groups	56.207	2	28.103	0.072	N.S
	Within Groups	116697.460	297	92.921		
	Total	**34781.450**	**299**			

INFERENCE

From the above table, it is clear that the obtained F value (0.072) is lower than the table value (3.03) at 0.05 level of significance.

It shows there is no significant difference between the mean scores of Self esteem amonghigher secondary studentsbased on Type of Management. Hence the **hypothesis 11 is accepted.**

INFLUENCE OF TYPE OF FAMILY ON SELF-ESTEEM

Hypothesis – 12

There is no significant difference between the mean scores of Self-Esteem among higher secondary students based on Type of Family.

TABLE.9.12: Showing the significant difference between the mean scores of Self-Esteem with respect to Type of Family

Variable	Type of Family	Number of cases	Mean	S.D	CR Value	LS
Self esteem	Joint	73	145.84	19.69	1.24	N.S
	Nuclear	227	142.53	19.88		

INFERENCE

From the table, it is clear that the obtained CR value (1.24) is lower than the table value (1.96) at 0.05 level of significance.

It shows that there is no significant difference between the mean scores of self esteem among higher secondary students with regard to type of family.

Hencethe **hypothesis 12 is accepted.**

INFLUENCE OF TYPE OF FATHER'S EDUCATIONAL QUALIFICATION ON SELF ESTEEM

Hypothesis – 13

There is no significant difference between the mean scores of Self-Esteem among higher secondary students based on Father's Qualification

TABLE.9.13: Showing ANOVA for Self -Esteem of Higher Secondary Students based on Father's Educational Qualification

Variable		Sum of Squares	df	Mean Squares	'F' Value	L.S
Self- Esteem	Between Groups	5354.008	2	2677.004	7.14	0.01
	Within Groups	111399.659	297	375.083		
	Total	116753.667	299			

INFERENCE

From the table, it is clear that the obtained F value (7.14) is higher than the table value (2.59) at 0.01 level of significance.

Itshows thatthere is significant difference between the means score self-esteem among higher secondary students. with regard to Father's Educational Qualification.

Further analysis have been made to find the difference among father's educational qualification.

TABLE.9.13 (A) Showing the Mean, S.D and C.R value for Self-Esteem of Higher Secondary Students based on Father's Educational Qualification.

Variable	Father's Educational Qulification	F	Mean	Std Deviation	C.R Value	L.S
Self- Esteem	Uneducated Vsn School	120	43.38	8.34	3.336	0.01
		119	40.28	5.77		
	School Vs College	119	40.28	5.77	0 .577	N.S
		121	39.82	6.94		
	College Vs Uneducated	121	39.82	6.94	3.59	0.01
		119	43.38	8.34		

INFERENCE

From the above table following inferences have been made.

In the first case, the calculated value (3.33) is greater than the table value (2.58) at 0.01 level of significance. It shows that there is significant difference between mean scores of Self-Esteem of the higher secondary students based on Father's Educational Qualification.(Uneducated VS School)

In the second case, the calculated value (0.577) is lower than the table value (1.96) at 0.05 level of significance.Itshows that there is no significant difference betweenmean scores of Self-Esteem of the higher secondary students based on Father's Educational Qualification. (School VS College)

In the third case, the calculated value (3.59) is higher than the expected table value (2.58) at 0.01 level of significance. It shows that there is significant difference between mean scores of Self-Esteem of the higher secondary students based on Father's Educational Qualification. (College VS Uneducated)

Hence, **Hypothesis 13** is partially verified.

This verification shows the Self-Esteem of higher secondary students is high whose Father's Uneducated.

INFLUENCE OF MOTHER'S EDUCATIONAL QUALIFICATION ON SELF ESTEEM

Hypothesis – 14

There is no significant difference between the mean scores of Self-Esteem among higher secondary students based on Mother's Qualification

TABLE 9.14: Showing ANOVA for Self-Esteem of Higher Secondary Students based on Mother's Educational Qualification.

Variable		Sum of Squares	df	Mean Squares	'F' Value	L.S
Self- Esteem	Between Groups	3713.817	2	1856.908	4.879	0.01
	Within Groups	113039.850	297	380.606		
	Total	116753.667	299			

INFERENCE

From the table, it is clear that the obtained F value (4.879) is higher than the table value (4.68) at 0.05 level of significance.

It shows that there is no significant difference between the mean scores of Self esteem among higher secondary studentswith regard to Mother's Educational Qualification.

Further analysis have been made to check the difference among various mother's educational status.

TABLE 9.14 (A): Showing the Mean, S.D and C.R value for Self-Esteem of Higher Secondary Students based on Mother's Educational Qualification.

Variable	Mother's Educational Qualification	F	Mean	Std Deviation	C.R Value	L.O.S
Self- Esteem	Uneducated Vs School	93	39.42	5.64	0 .010	N.S
		126	42.87	7.73		
	School Vs College	126	42.87	7.73	2.26	0.05
		141	40.77	7.48		
	College Vs Uneducated	141	40.77	7.47	1 48	N.S
		93	39.42	5.64		

NFERENCE

From the above table following inference have been made.

In the first case, the calculated value (0.010) is lower than table value (1.96) at 0.05 level of significance. It shows that there is no significant difference between mean scores Self-Esteem of the higher secondary students based on Mother's Educational Qualification (Uneducated VS School)

In the second case, the calculated value (2.26) is higher than the table value (1.96) at 0.05 level of significance.It shows that there is significant difference between mean scores of Self-Esteem of the higher secondary students based on Mother's Educational Qualification. (School VS College VS)

In the third case, the calculated value (1.48) is lower than the expected table value (1.96) at 0.05 level of significance. It shows that there is no significant difference between mean scores Self-Esteem of the higher secondary students based on Mother's Educational Qualification (College VS Uneducated)

Hence, **Hypothesis 14** is partially verified.

This verification shows the Self-Esteem of the higher secondary students is high whose Mother's or School.

INFLUENCEOF BIRTH ORDERONSOCIAL INTELLIGENCE

Hypothesis – 15

There is no significant difference between the mean scores of Self-Esteem among higher secondary students based on Birth Order

TABLE.9.15: Showing ANOVA for Self Esteem of
Higher Secondary Students based on Father's Educational Qualification

Variable		Sum of Squares	df	Mean Squares	'F' Value	L.S
Self esteem	Between Groups	6007.883	2	3003.942	8.056	0.01
	Within Groups	110745.784	297	372.881		
	Total	116753.667	299			

IINFERENCE

From the table, it is clear that the obtained F value (8.056) higher than the table value (4.68) at 0.01 level of significance. It shows that there is significant difference between the mean scores of Self-esteem among higher secondary student with regard to birth order.

Further calculation have been made to clear the difference among various birth orders.

TABLE.9.15 (A): Showing the Mean, S.D and C.R value for Self-Esteem of Higher Secondary Students based on Birth Order

Variable	Birth Order	F	Mean	Std Deviation	C.R Value	L.S
Self Esteem	First Vs Middle	78	43.51	8.55	2.76	0.01
		148	40.72	6.47		
	Middle vs Last	148	40.72	6.47	0.577	N.S
		134	40.27	7.02		
	Last vs First	134	40.27	7.02	2.99	0.01
		78	43.51	8.55		

INFERENCE

From the above table following inference have been made.

In the first case, the calculated value (2.76) is higher than table value (2.58) at 0.01 level of significance. Its hows that there is significant difference between mean scores of Self-Esteem of the higher secondary students based on Birth Order. (First VS Middle)

In the second case, the calculated value (0.577) is lower than the table value (1.96) at 0.05 level of significance. It that there is no significant difference between mean scores of Self-Esteem of the higher secondary students based on Birth Order. (Middle VS Last)

In the third case, the calculated value (2.99) is more than the expected table value (2.58) at 0.01 level of significance. It that there is significant difference between mean scores of Self-Esteem of the higher secondary students based on Birth Order. (Last VS First)

Hence, **Hypothesis 15** is partially verified.

From this verification students who born in first order in their birth have high self-esteem than other orders respectively.

INFLUENCE OF FAMILY MONTHLY INCOME SELF-ESTEEM

Hypothesis – 16

There is no significant difference between the mean scores of Self-Esteem among higher secondary students based on Family Monthly Income

TABLE.9.16: Showing ANOVA for Self Esteem of Higher Secondary Students based Onfamily Monthly Income

Variable		Sum of Squares	df	Mean Squares	'F' Value	L.S
Self esteem	Between Groups	1398.838	3	466.279	1.196	N.S
	Within Groups	115354.829	296	389.712		
	Total	116753.667	299			

IINFERENCE

From the table, it is clear that the obtained F value (1.196) lower than the table value (3.03) at 0.05 level of significance. Itshows that there is no significant difference between the mean scores of Self-esteem among higher secondary student with regard to family monthly income.

Hence, **Hypothesis 16** is accepted.

CORRELATION BETWEEN SOCIAL INTELLIGENCE AND SELF- ESTEEM

Hypothesis 17

There is no significant correlation between the Social Intelligence and Self-Esteem among higher secondary students.

TABLE.9.17: Correlation between Social Intelligence and Self-Esteem among Higher Secondary Students

Variable	N	Correlation	L.S
Social Intelligence Vs Self esteem	300	0.388	0.01

INFERENCE

From the above table, it is clear that there is a significant relationship betweensocial intelligence and self-esteem among higher secondary students.

It is also noted that there is positive correlation between Social Intelligence and Self-Esteem.

CONCLUSION

This chapter explains the analysis of data, testing of hypotheses and interpretation of the data. A brief report of the research study together with the major findings, educational implications and the suggestions for further research has been presented in succeeding chapter.

❐

10

Summary Finding Conclusion

"Research data becomes meaningful in the process of beinganalyzed and interpreted"

- George J. Mouly (1964).

The present chapter provides a brief summary of the entire study and it also gives the interpretation of results ensuing from the statistical analysis of date presented in the previous chapter. The implications along with suggestions for implicating the study or for investigation of other closely related problem in other setting and with different samples and tools are also presented.

STATEMENT OF THE PROBLEM

"Social Intelligence and Self Esteem among Higher Secondary Students"

OPERATIONAL DEFINITIONS

Social Intelligence

By this investigator means the total score obtained in the social intelligence inventory prepared and standardized by Dr .N.K. chanda (1990)

Socialization involves the complementary process of individualization and along with social development the child also develops "social intelligence". A positive or favorable self-esteem towards one's life, help in developing social intelligence.

Self-Esteem

Self-esteem is the individual's way of looking at one's abilities and personality it also signifies his way of thinking, feeling and behaving.Self-esteem is one of the aspects of personality pattern, and it governs the individual's characteristic reaction to people and situations.

By this the investigator means the scores obtained from the Self-Esteem Inventory (1989).

OBJECTIVES OF THE STUDY

The following objectives are set in the present study.

1. To find out the level of Social Intelligence of higher secondary students.
2. To find out the level of Self-Esteem among higher secondary students.
3. To find out whether there is any significant difference between mean scores of Social Intelligence of higher secondary students based on Gender.
4. To find out whether there is any significant difference between mean scores of Social Intelligence of higher secondary students based on Type of Management.
5. To find out whether there is any significant difference between mean scores of Social Intelligence of higher secondary students based on Type of Family.
6. To find out whether there is any significant difference between mean scores of Social Intelligence of higher secondary students based on Father's Qualification.
7. To find out whether there is any significant difference between the mean scores of Social Intelligence of higher secondary students based on Mother's Qualification
8. To find out whether there is any significant difference between the mean scores of Social Intelligence of higher secondary students based on Birth Order.
9. To find out whether there is any significant difference between the mean scores of Social Intelligence of higher secondary students based on Family Monthly Income.
10. To find out whether there is any significant difference between the mean scores of Self-Esteem among higher secondary students Based on Gender.

11. To find out whether there is any significant difference between the mean scores of Self-Esteem among higher Secondary students based on Type of Management.
12. To find out whether there is any significant difference between the mean scores of Self-Esteem among higher secondary students based on Type of Family.
13. To find out whether there is any significant difference between the mean scores of Self-Esteem among higher secondary students based on Father's Qualification.
14. To find out whether there is any significant difference between the mean scores of Self-Esteem among higher secondary students based on Mother's Qualification.
15. To find out whether there is any significant difference between the mean scores of Self-Esteem among higher secondary students based on Birth Order
16. To find out whether there is any significant difference between the mean scores of Self-Esteem among higher secondary students based on Family Monthly Income.
17. To find out whether there is any significant correlation among the variables of Social Intelligence and Self-Esteem among higher secondary students.

HYPOTHESES OF THE STUDY

The researcher has formulated the following hypotheses pertaining to the present study.

1. The levels of Social Intelligence among the higher secondary students is moderate in nature.
2. The level of self-esteem among higher secondary students is moderate in nature.
3. There is no significant difference between the mean scores of Social Intelligence among higher secondary students based on Gender.
4. There is no significant difference between the mean scores of Social Intelligence among higher secondary students based on Type of Management.
5. There is no significant difference between the mean scores of Social Intelligence among higher secondary students based on Type of Family.
6. There is no significant difference between the mean scores of Social Intelligence among higher secondary students based on Father's Qualification.

7. There is no significant difference between the mean scores of Social Intelligence among higher secondary students based on Mother's Qualification.
8. There is no significant difference between the mean scores of Social Intelligence among higher secondary students based on Birth Order.
9. There is no significant difference between the mean scores of Social Intelligence among higher secondary students based on Family Monthly Income.
10. There is no significant difference between the mean scores of Self-Esteem among higher secondary students based on Gender.
11. There is no significant difference between the mean scores of Self-Esteem among higher secondary students based on Type of Management.
12. There is no significant difference between the mean scores of Self-Esteem among higher secondary students based on Type of Family.
13. There is no significant difference between the mean scores of Self-Esteem among higher secondary students based on Father's Qualification.
14. There is no significant difference between the mean scores of Self-Esteem among higher secondary students based on Mother's Qualification.
15. There is no significant difference between the mean scores of Self-Esteem among higher secondary students based on Birth Order.
16. There is no significant difference between the mean scores of Self-Esteem among higher secondary students based on Family Monthly Income.
17. There is no significant correlation between the Social Intelligence and Self-Esteem among higher secondary students.

TOOLS USED

To collect the pertinent data for the present investigation, standardized tools have been employed to quantify the variables involved in the study.

The investigator has used the following tools for the data collection. They are listed below:

- Personal data sheet consists of details like Gender, Type of Management, Type of Family, Father's Qualification, Mother's Qualification, Birth Order and Family Monthly Income.
- Social Intelligence Scale prepared was constructed by Dr. N.K. Chandha(1990)
- Self EsteemM.S.Prasad, G.P.Thakar(1989)

MAJOR FINDINGS

1. It was found the level of Social Intelligence among the higher secondary students is moderate in nature.
2. It was found thelevel of self-esteem among higher secondary students is moderate in nature.
3. It was found there is no significant difference between the mean scores of Social Intelligence among higher secondary students based on Gender.
4. It was foundthere is no significant difference between the mean scores of Social Intelligence among higher secondary students based on Type of Management.
5. It was foundthere is no significant difference between the mean scores of Social Intelligence among higher secondary students based on Type of Family.
6. It was foundthere is no significant difference between the mean scores of Social Intelligence among higher secondary students based on Father's Qualification.
7. It was foundthere is no significant difference between the mean scores of Social Intelligence among higher secondary students based on Mother's Qualification.
8. It was foundthere is no significant difference between the mean scores of Social Intelligence among higher secondary students based on Birth Order.
9. It was foundthere is no significant difference between the mean scores of Social Intelligence among higher secondary students based on Family Monthly Income.
10. It was foundthere is no significant difference between the mean scores of Self-Esteem among higher secondary students based on Gender.
11. It was foundthere is no significant difference between the mean scores of Self-Esteem among higher secondary students based on Type of Management.
12. It was foundthere is no significant difference between the mean scores of Self-Esteem among higher secondary students based on Type of Family.
13. It was foundthere is no significant difference between the mean scores of Self-Esteem among higher secondary students based on Father's Qualification.
14. It was found there is no significant difference between the mean scores of Self-Esteem among higher secondary students based on Mother's Qualification.

15. It was foundthere is no significant difference between the mean scores of Self-Esteem among higher secondary students based on Birth Order.
16. It was foundthere is no significant difference between the mean scores of Self-Esteem among higher secondary students based on Family Monthly Income.
17. It was foundthere is no significant correlation between the Social Intelligence and Self-Esteem among higher secondary students.

EDUCATIONAL IMPLICATIONS

Development of social intelligence among school students is a different complex task. In school there should be lot of scope for participation in different programme, curricular and co-curricular activities. Children should be encouraged to participate in all programmes, since they offer scope for developing Flexible manner, Tolerance and self-evaluation ability among the individuals.

The findings of the present investigation is important for the improvement in the quality of education. Self-esteem is also quality which play major role in their life. Co-curricular activities should also be used for developing social intelligence and self-esteem. If the self esteem whereas in the present study it is revealed that the students have moderate level of self esteem.

DELIMITATIONS OF THE STUDY

The present study had the following delimitations

- In this study the investigator focuses only on Social Intelligence and Self-Esteem though there are other factors that may also influence the student behavior.
- Data collection is restricted to Chennai District only
- The present study is restricted exclusively to higher secondary Plus One students.
- The investigator has selected only three type of school viz., government, government aided and private.
- The sample is restricted to 300.

SUGGESTIONS FOR FURTHUER RESEARCH

Some suggestions with regard to possibilities of the research in the field of education are offered with a view of stimulate prospective research workers in this area.

- The study could be extended to College Students.
- The present study has done only in some schools at Chennai District; similar study comprising different districts can be attempted.

- The sample size is restricted to 300 School Students in the present study. It can be done by including more number of schools students.

CONCLUSION

Thus in this chapter the researcher has concluded the whole research work based on the findings of the research the researcher has framed the educational implications for improvement. Further possible research studies are also mentioned in this chapter.

❐

11

The Problem and its Perspectives

"Education according to Indian tradition is not merely a means to earn a living nor is it only a nursery of thought or a school of citizenship, it is initiation into the life of spirit, a training of the human soul in the pursuit of truth and practice of virtue, it is a second birth of mankind -John dewey.

The word education is often used to refer solely to formal education. However, it covers a range of experiences, from formal learning to the building of understanding through day to day experiences. Ultimately all that we experience serves as a form of education.

Education will give to the individual a strong and healthy body helps him in building up his character and attains self mastery and supplies him with good opportunities of discovering and developing and developing harmoniously his natural abilities.

THE CONCEPT OF EMOTIONAL COMPETENCE

The concept of emotional competence is rooted in understanding emotions as normal, useful aspects of being human. Anger is a reaction to aggression and gives a person the strength to repel the aggression. Grief is a reaction to abandonment or feeling unloved and it has the effect of eliciting sympathetic responses from others. Fear is a response to danger and has a clear physiological effect or heightening our senses and speeding up out reaction.

MEANING OF EMOTIONAL COMPETENCE

(Emotional competence refers to one's ability to express or release one's ability to express or release one's inner feelings (emotions). It implies a case around others and determines one's ability effectively and successfully leads and express. (1) It is described as the essential social skills to recognize, interpret, and respond constructively to emotions in yourself and others.

THE NATURE OF EMOTIONS

Feeling and emotions are strictly subjective, individual, personal, intimate experiences. Feelings are always present in conscious liking and denote states of satisfaction or dissatisfaction, liking or disliking anything. Emotions are more complex than feelings and involve feelings, impulses to action and adjustment, and bodily changes and excitement. In order to understand the educational significance of emotions and their development, it is essential to lay down criteria for distinguishing between emotional and non-emotional experience.

1. Emotion is stirred-up condition involving disturbance, excitement, conflict or tension in behavior. In an emotional situation, some stimulus arouses or stirs emotions into action.
2. An emotion is brought into action by the perception of some stimulus. Psychologically it is a complex experience involving perception and widespread characteristic bodily changes in the action of muscles, glands and the automatic nervous system.
3. Every emotional state involves an impulse to action. There is a drive toward some kind of adjustment, to obtain satisfaction, to effect destruction or escape or to gratify a desire. The emotion subsides to the extent to which adjustments are achieved.

EFFECTS OF EMOTION

1. Emotions provide energy to an individual to face a particular situation.
2. Emotions work as motivators of our behavior.
3. Emotions influence our adjustment in the society.
4. High emotional conditions disturb the mental equilibrium of an individual.
5. High emotional conditions disturb the reasoning and thinking of an individual.

EMOTIONAL COMPETENCE

PERSONAL COMPETENCE

(B) SELF AWARENESS
- Emotional awareness
- Accurate self-assessment
- Self-confidence

(B) SELF REGULATION
- Self control
- Trust worthiness
- Conscientiousness
- Adaptability
- Innovation

(C) MOTIVATION
- Achievement Drive
- Commitment
- Initiative
- Optimism

SOCIAL COMPETENCE

(A) EMPATHY
- Understanding others
- Developing others
- Service orientation
- Leveraging Diversity
- Political Awareness

(B) SOCIAL SKILLS
- Influence
- Communication
- Conflict management
- Leadership
- Change catalyst
- Building Bonds
- Collaboration and co operation
- Team capabilities

PERSONAL COMPETENCE

Self-Awareness

A. **Emotional Awareness:** Recognizing one's emotions and their effects. People with this competence:
   - know which emotions they are feeling and why
   - realize the links between their feelings and what they think, do, and say
   - recognize how their feelings affect their performance and
   - have a guiding awareness of their values and goals

B. **Accurate Self-Assessment:** knowing one's strength and limits. People with this competence are:
   - aware of their strengths and weaknesses
   - reflective, learning from experience
   - open to candid feedback. New perspectives, continuous learning and self-development

- able to show a sense of humor and perspective about themselves.

C. **Self-Confidence:** sureness about one's self-worth and capabilities. People with this competence:
- present themselves with self-assurance; have "presence"
- can voice views that are unpopular and go out on a limb for what is right
- are decisive, able to make sound decisions despite uncertainties and pressures

SELF-REGULATION

A. **Self-Control:** Managing disruptive emotions and impulses. People with this competence:
- manage their impulsive feelings and distressing emotions well
- stay composed, positive, and unflappable even in trying moments
- think clearly and stay focused under pressure

B. **Trustworthiness:** Maintaining standards of honesty and integrity. People with this competence:
- act ethically and are above reproach
- build trust through their reliability and authenticity
- admit their own mistakes and confront unethical actions in others
- take tough, principled stands even if they are unpopular

C. **Conscientiousness:** Taking responsibility for personal performance. People with this competence:
- meet commitments and keep promises
- hold themselves accountable for meeting their objectives
- are organized and careful in their work

D. **Adaptability:** flexibility in handling change. People with this competence:
- smoothly handle multiple demands, shifting priorities, and rapid change
- adapt their responses and tactics to fit fluid circumstances
- are flexible in how they see events

E. **Innovativeness:** being comfortable with and open to novel ideas and new information people with this competence:
- seek out fresh ideas from a wide variety of sources
- entertain original solutions to problems
- generate new ideas
- take fresh perspectives and risks in their thinking

SELF-MOTIVATION

A. **Achievement Drive:** striving to improve or meet a standard of excellence. People with this competence:
- are results-oriented, with a high drive to meet their objectives and standards
- set challenging goals and take calculated risks
- pursue information to reduce uncertainty and find ways to do better
- learn how to improve their performance

B. **Commitment**: Aligning with the goals of the group or organization. People with this competence:
- readily make personal or group sacrifices to meet a larger organizational goal
- find a sense of purpose in the large mission
- use the group's core values in making decisions and clarifying choices
- actively seek out opportunities to fulfill the group's mission

C. **Initiative:** Readiness to act on opportunities. People with this competence;
- are ready to seize opportunities
- pursue goals beyond what's required or expected of them
- cut through red tape and bend the rules when necessary to get the job done
- mobilize others through unusual, enterprising efforts.

D. **Optimism:** Persistence in pursuing goals despite obstacle and setbacks. People with this competence:
- persist in seeking goals despite obstacles and setbacks
- operate from hop of success rather than fear of failure
- see setbacks as due to manageable circumstance rather than a personal flaw

SOCIAL COMPETENCE

Social Awareness

A. **Empathy:** sensing other's feelings and perspective, and taking an active interest in their concerns. People with this competence:
- are attentive to emotional cues and listen well
- show sensitivity and understand other's perspectives
- help out based on understanding other people's needs and feelings

B. Service Orientation: Anticipating, recognizing, and meeting customers' needs. People with this competence.

- understand customers' needs and match them to services or products
- seek ways to increase customers' satisfaction and loyalty
- gladly offer appropriate assistance
- grasp a customer's perspective, acting as a trusted advisor

C. Developing Others: Sensing what others need in order to develop, and bolstering their abilities. People with this competence:

- acknowledge and reward people's strengths, accomplishments, and development
- offer useful feedback and identify people's need for development
- mentor, give timely coaching, and offer assignments that challenge and grow a person's skills.

D. Leveraging Diversity: cultivating opportunities through diverse people. People with this competence:

- respect and relate well to people from varied backgrounds
- understand diverse worldviews and are sensitive to group differences
- see diversity as opportunity, creating an environment where diverse people can thrive
- challenge bias and intolerance

E. Political awareness: Reading a group's emotional currents and power relationships. People with this competence:

- accurately read key power relationship
- detect crucial social networks
- understand the forces that shape views and actions of clients, customers, or competitors
- accurately read situations and organizational and external realities.

SOCIAL SKILLS

A. Influence: Wielding effective tactics for persuasion. People with this competence:

- are skilled at persuasion
- fine-tune presentations to appeal to the listener
- use complex strategies like indirect influence to build consensus and support
- orchestrate dramatic events to effectively make a point

B. Communication: Sending clear and convincing messages. People with this competence

- are effective in give-and–take registering emotional cues in attuning their message
- deal with difficult issues straightforwardly
- listen well, seek mutual understanding, and welcome sharing of information fully
- foster open communication and stay receptive to bad news as well as good

C. **Leadership**: inspiring and guiding groups and people. People with this competence:
- articulate and arouse enthusiasm for a shared vision and mission
- step forward to lead as needed, regardless of position
- huide the performance of others while holding them accountable
- lead by example

D. **Change Catalyst**: initiating or managing change. People with this competence:
- recognize the need for change and remove barriers
- challenge the status quo to acknowledge the need for change
- champion the change and enlist others in its pursuit
- model the change expected of others

E. **Conflict Management**: Negotiating and resolving disagreements. People with this competence:
- handle difficult people and tense situations with diplomacy and tact
- depot potential conflict, bring disagreements into the open, and help deescalate
- encourage debate and open discussion
- orchestrate win-win solutions

F. **Building bonds**: Nurturing instrumental relationships. People with this competence:
- cultivate and maintain extensive informal network
- seek out relationships that are mutually beneficial
- build rapport and keep others in the loop
- make and maintain personal friendship among work associates

G. **Collaboration and Cooperation**: working with others towards shared goals. People with this competence:
- balance a focus on task with attention to relationships
- collaborate, sharing plans, information, and resources
- promote a friendly, cooperative climate
- spot and nurture opportunities for collaboration

H. **Team Capabilities**: creating group synergy in pursuing collective goals. People with this competence:
- model team qualities like respect, helpfulness, and cooperation
- draw all members into active and enthusiastic participation
- build team identity, esprit de corps, and commitment

CRITERIA FOR ASSESSING EMOTIONAL COMPETENCY

- An emotional competent person can express their emotionality freely, where and when appropriate and can hold on to feeling for later expression, can tolerate the expression of feeling including distress in other people.
- An emotional competent person discovers the main elements of their traumatic early experience and appreciates how they influence adult behavior.
- An emotional competent person actively seeks to identify and own projection/displacement, transference/ counter transference.
- An emotional competent person will have adequate appreciation of the contribution of expression, both covert and overt, to feeling and emotions.
- An emotional competent person can supportively confront unaware behavior in others.
- An emotional competent person can cathartically release strong emotion.
- An emotional competent person can transmute tense emotion through choosing to make a shift in conscious.
- An emotional competent person takes responsibility for continuing to develop and sustain their emotional competence.

THE CONCEPT OF LEADERSHIP PREFERENCE

Leadership has been described as "a process of social influence in which one person can enlist the aid and support of others in the accomplishment of a common task" For example, some understand a leader simply as somebody whom people follow, or as somebody who guides or directs others, while others define leadership as "organizing a group of people to achieve a common goal". Leadership is a process of influencing the behavior of others to work willingly and enthusiastically for achieving predetermined goals. Leadership is built on relationship. Leadership yocuses on purpose. Leadership is service oriented its main aim is to reach out and help others to became all that they can leader with social maturity foster a sense of solidarity and concern .A leader shapes and shares vision which gives point to the work of others-Charles handy (1992) Leadership and learning are indispensable to each other-John F.Kennady

DEFINITION OF LEADERSHIP

- "Leadership can be defined as the process of directing and influencing the task related activates of group members".

CHARACTERISTRICS OF A LEADERSHIP

Effective leadership should possess the following essential aspects:-

- motivating the team
- crating confidence among the team members
- building morale within the team
- fulfills certain pre determined objectives.
- functioning for a common goal
- maintains a good relationship with the followers.

IMPORTANCE OF LEADERSHIP

In every society there is a great demand for leaders, for its survival asks for better leaders, the insistence on the demand for leaders is evidently due to pressing needs of the environment. They need to be talent for leading the particular group. Everybody cannot lead and every person cannot effectively handle organize human relationship, keeping this in view, leadership problem occur each and every society. Leaders try to influence the behavior of others for attainment of some special goals and objectives. Leadership behavior is in demand in various fields of life situations social, political cultural, educational etc.

Leadership is therefore a very important feature of many spheres of human activity and it can have far reaching effect on the zeal and activities of the group and can promote or retard activities in administration, battlefield, industries and politics. Leadership has been defined as may ways some of the definition are given below.

- Interpersonal influence directed through communication towards goal attainment
- An act that causes others to act or respond in a shared direction
- The art of influencing people by persuasion or example to follow a time of action
- The principle dynamic force that motivate and coordinate the organization in accomplishing its objectives

Preference for a particular style of leadership brings along with certain amount of joy and satisfaction to the leader, this sense of satisfaction stems from such factors as power, prestige. The opportunity to help others with high involvement and the opportunity to control resources at other times for having chosen to be a leader in one's own perfection style one has to face a number of frustrations such as insufficient authority dealing with human problems and too much organizational politics.

STATEMENT OF THE PROBLEM

The present study is entitled as "Influence of Emotional Competence on Leadership Preference among High School Students".

THE OPERATIONAL DEFINITION

Emotional Competence

Emotional competence is the demonstration of self-efficacy in emotion-eliciting social transaction **BY SARNI 1999.**

In the present study, it is measured by Emotional Competence Assessment Scale [ECAS] prepared by Suresh Kumar. M and Fulton Paiva.J.S

Leadership Preference

REUTER has defined leadership in the following words, 'Leadership is an ability to persuade or direct man without use of prestige or power of formal office or eternal circumstance'.

In the presents study, it is constructed by L.I. Bhushan and validated by the investigator.

High School Students

In the present study, high school students studying under Tamil Nadu State Board High School Students has been considered.

OBJECTIVES OF THE STUDY

The objectives framed in the present study are listed below:

1. To find out the level of emotional competence of high school students.
2. To find out the level of leadership preference of high school students.
3. To find out whether there is any significant difference between the mean score of Emotional competence of high school students.

   Gender : Male / Female
   Type of management : Govt /Govt aided/
   Private Birth order : First born/Middle
   born/Last born
   Type of family : Nuclear/ joint

4. To find out whether there is any significant difference between the mean score of Leadership preference of high school students.

- Gender
- Type of management
- Birth order
- Type of family

5. To find out whether there is any significant correlation between the Emotional competence and Leadership preference of high school students.

NEED FOR STUDY

Education is very important to everyone to lead a successful life. Emotions have a great effect on student's academic progress. Every individual is able to say, think, feel and tackle their problem under all circumstances. Emotional Competence helps person appropriate strategies for identifying and acting on their desires, needs and opinions. Emotional Competence is a broad approach that can be applied to many different personal, academic and work situations.

The personal attributes of leaders, understanding this approach was the assumption that some people are natural leaders who are endowed with certain trait not possessed by other people, the so called 'great man' theory attempted to describe leadership preference as innate gifts that few were bestowed at birth. Early leadership theories attributed a leader's success to the possession of extraordinary ability such as tried less, energy institution and foresight.

Emotional Competence on Leadership Preference enabled the students to put more into reality, to express confidently and courageously.

Hence the present investigation is undertaken to find out whether there is any significant influence of Emotional Competence on Leadership Preference among High School Students.

LIMITATIONS OF THE STUDY

The present investigation has the following limitations:-

- The students has been limited to Vellore district only
- The sample size is limited to 300 school students
- The study is restricted to 4 schools only.

CONCLUSION

The problem of the present study has been discussed briefly in this chapter the terms operationally defined in this study have been reviewed thereoretically from the related literature available so as to give a broadened theoretical perspective, in this light of which appropriate hypothesis could be framed and tested. A detailed discussion of the related literature follows in the next chapter.

❒

12

Review of Related Literature

The survey of related studies implies locating studying and evaluating reports of relevant researches study of published articles, going through related portions of encyclopedias and research abstracts, study of pertinent pages out of comprehensive books on the subject and going through related manuscripts if any.

STUDIES RELATED TO EMOTIONAL COMPETENCE

MEGREW AND SCOTT (1989), investigated the relation between adaptive and maladaptive Behavior and other important human competence constructs in the context of a model of personal competence. It was concluded that adoptive and maladaptive behaviors weredistinct dimensions separate from, but related to, the dimensions of intelligence and physical competence. Support was also found for portions of Greenspan's model of personal competence which defines personal competence as a combination of the broad abilities of practical intelligence (adaptive behavior), emotional competence (maladaptive behavior), conceptual intelligence, physical competence and social intelligence.

BRAR (1992) studied social emotional competence of pre–school children: relationship to intelligence and maturity. Social-emotional competence (SEC) is considered a measure of an individual's total effectiveness in dealing with the environment. To verify empirically whether SEC depends on the intelligence and social maturity of young children, a study of 40 pre–school children was undertaken in India. A standardized intelligence test was administered to the children to assess SEC and social maturity. Children were observed in school and during home activities. Based on test and observation results, children were categorized into groups of high and low intelligence and into groups of high and low social maturity. Scores for the groups were compared with respect to four aspects of SEC: I) Self-confidence; ii) Autonomy-dependence; iii)Quality of social interactions; and IV) Coping techniques. Data indicated that children categorized in the high intelligence group scored significantly higher than children in the low intelligence group on all four aspects of SEC. Similarly, children categorized as high in social maturity scored significantly better than children categorized as low in social maturity on the four aspects of SEC. From these findings it was concluded that a child's level of intelligence and maturity contributes significantly to social and emotional competency.

GERNER.W (1996) conducted a study the purpose of which was to evaluate whether emotional understanding continues to impact children's social competence once they reach middle childhood. Thirty nine low-income third and fourth graders were administered three emotional knowledge tasks: (a) emotional roll taking, (b) knowledge of effective attributions, and (c) Knowledge of emotional display rules.

HUDANI (1997) found no significant difference between volunteers and non-volunteers in term of emotional competence. The results also showed that emotional competence was moderately correlated with neuroticism, psychoticism and extraversion dimensions of personality.

BHARADWAJ (1998) studied emotional competence in relation to early adolescent labourers and non-labourers of both the sexes andfound that female early adolescent labourers had greater emotional competence than female non- labourers. Male labourers have greater adequate expression and control of emotions than non-labors. An UJ (2000) found a positive and significant relationship between emotional maturity and intelligence of students, which implies that more intelligent a person is, more emotionally he is Kaur (2000) founda significant relationship between emotional maturity and school, home and psychological environment. However, no significant relationship was found between emotional maturity and physical environment.

JAGERS (2001) studied cultural integrity and social and emotional competence promotion: work notes on moral competence. The research describes evolving conceptual and programmatic efforts to promote African American children's social and emotional competencies. Determining the developmental imperatives for African American children is an essential step in crafting competence theory, research, and practice for this population. The concept of moral self-efficacy is offered as a bridge between moral emotions and moral behaviours. The school and community factors associated with moral behaviours are touched on, with particular attention to issues of power, authority, and oppression. Following this, some strategies for moral competence promotion in school and extended-hour contexts are presented. There is a focus on interweaving the foregoing insights with existing best practices in social and emotional learning.

PAMELA AND KIMBERLY (2001) conducted a study on emotional competence, emotion socialization and young children's peer-related social competence. In the study, the emotional competence measures included situation knowledge, children's explanations of emotions, and positivism of emotional expression during peer play, and emotional intensity. Results revealed that the emotional competence variables were meaningfully related to the peer variables and that, for non-constructive anger reactions, maternal reports of anger explained unique variance. Results are discussed in terms of how emotional competence and emotion socialization contribute to peer behaviour and the importance of designing and implementing affective intervention programmes for young children and their families.

FRIEDMAN SARA R, RAPPORT LISA J (2003), social and emotional competence were evaluated using self-report and behavioral measures in adults with attention-deficit/hyperactivity disorder (ADHD) and controls. Adults with ADHD viewed themselves as less socially competent but more sensitive toward violations of social forms than controls. Films depicting emotional interactions were used to assess linguistic properties of free recall and perceived emotional intensity. Although adults with ADHD used more words to describe the scenes, they used fewer emotion-related words, despite rating the emotions depicted as more intense than did controls. In contrast, no group difference for words depicting social or cognitive processes were observed. Overall, adults with ADHD appear more aware of their problems in social versus emotional skills. Findings may have implications for improving the psychosocial functioning of these adults.

BOHNERTETAL. (2003) studied emotional competence and aggressive behaviourin school age children. They examined emotional competence in 87 children, aged 7–10 years, who varied with respect to reports of aggressive behaviour to determine whether individual differences in emotional competence characterize children with higher levels of aggressive behaviour. Emotional competence was assessed during a 1-hr lab visit that included -i) Anobservational period consisting of a modified disappointment paradigm, ii) Assessment of cognitive and language abilities, and iii) 2 structured emotion interviews. Children with higher levels of aggressive behaviour exhibited more intense and frequent expressions of anger, both as reported by mothers and as observed during the disappointment paradigm. Less sophisticated ability to identify the causes of emotion also characterized children with higher levels of aggressive behaviour. Gender moderated the relation between aggressive behaviour and type of emotion.

LINSEYANDCOLWELL (2003) studied preschooler's emotional competence: links to pretend and physical play. Data were collected from 44 preschool children (22 boys, 22 girls; 34 European American, 2 African American, 6 Asian, 2 Hispanic). Children participated in emotion understanding interviews. Mothers rated children's emotion regulation ability and teachers rated children emotional competence with peers. In addition, the amount of children's pretend and physical play during same-sex dyadic play with a friend from their preschool classroom was assessed. Findings suggest that emotion regulation and emotion understanding make unique contributions to teacher ratings of children's emotional competence with peers; however, different patterns of associations were found for boys.

SARAH W. BLACKSTONE, DAVID P. WILKINS (2006), explored the Importance of emotional Competence in Children with Complex Communication Needs. Research has shown that children with significant language impairments lag behind their typically developing peers in commu-nicative and emotional competence. The research also explores the importance of emotional competence in children with complex communication needs.

ALYSIA Y. BLANDON, SUSAN D. CALKINS (2007), the longitudinal associations between maternal parenting behavior and toddler risk with children's emotional and social competence were examined during the transition to kindergarten, in a sample of 253 children. Toddler risk was characterized by early externalizing behavior and poor emotion regulation skills. The interactions among material parenting behavior and toddler risk. There were some significant interactions, although the pattern of results was not consistent across all competence outcomes. Maternal parenting behavior was not directly associated with children's emotional and social competence. In some instances, maternal control has differential implications for children's emotional and social competence dependent upon the child's level of early risk and maternal positive parenting.

ALISON L.MILLER, SARAH E.FINE, (2007), examined relations between three facets of emotional competence: emotion knowledge, level of negative emotion expression, and emotion regulation of low income preschoolers(N=60) and their associations with indicators of classroom adjustment. Emotion knowledge was positively related to positive emotion regulation but was not related to negative emotion expression or negative deregulation. Negative emotion expression related to emotion regulation variables in expected directions. Negative emotion expression was associated with aggression and social skills after covering verbal ability, age, and emotion knowledge. Negative deregulation was related in expected directions to aggression, anxiety, and social skills after covering verbal ability, age, emotion knowledge, and negative emotion expression. Positive emotion regulation was related negatively to anxiety and positively to social skills after covering all other variables in the model. Results were discussed with regard to using the emotional competence domain to understand how emotion processing relates to early childhood adjustment.

LYNN R. OFFERMANN, JAMES R. BAILEY (2007), studied the relative contributions of emotional competence and cognitive ability to individual and team performance, team-member attitudes, and leadership perceptions were examined. Focusing on emotional competencies, it was predicted that, although both cognitive ability and emotional competence would predict performance, cognitive ability would account for more variance on individual tasks, whereas emotional competence would account for more variance in team performance and attitudes. Emotional competence would be positively related to team attitudes and to both leader emergence and effectiveness. Using a sample of undergraduate business majors who completed tasks alone and as members of teams, the results generally supported the hypotheses.

BEGEER ETAL.(2008) studied emotional competence in children with autism: Diagnostic criteria and empirical evidence. The researchers reported four aspects of emotional competence that are important to children's daily social functioning (expression, perception, responding, and understanding), differentiated between mentally retarded and normally intelligent children and adolescents with and without ASD in natural and structured contexts. On various accounts, the emotional impairments of children with ASD that are found in scientific studies

KATJA PETROWSKI, (2008), studied children's social-emotional competence development. The social-emotional competence of 65 Asian-American and Latin-American children was observed at the beginning and the end of their kindergarten year. Initially, significant differences existed among these ethnic groups in respect to moral reasoning. Furthermore, the male children showed more deregulated aggression but the female children implemented more moral reasoning than their male counterparts. These ethnic specificities did not disappear over the course of the year. In addition, a significant change in avoidance strategies as well as expressed emotions in the narrative took place over the course of one year. Ethnic specificity in social-emotional competence does exist independent of gender at the beginning as well as well as at the end of the kindergarten year in a multi-ethnic kindergarten classroom. Reported on the quality of their peer relations and teachers provided ratings of the children's pro-social behavior. Results revealed that children's attribution of aggression and denial were positively related to their reports of negative peer interactions. Children's pro-social behaviour was positively predicated by emotional roll-taking ability and knowledge of pro-social display rules. These findings underscored by importance of emotional knowledge for children's social functioning across early and middle childhood.

SHARI L. KIDWELL, LISA D. HINKLE (2008), examined attachment in association with preschooler's emotional functioning among 54 predominantly low-income families living in Appalachia. Attachment was assessed t age 4 years using the Strange Situation (Blehar, Water, & Wall, 1978) and classified with the PAA (Crittenden, 2004). Emotional competence was measured via an interview about children's memories for six emotions, rated in terms of both emotion understanding and regulation. Parent-teachers and self-reports of children's internalizing and externalizing symptoms were also completed. Questionnaires and interviews assessed socioeconomic risk and parental symptoms and negative childhood experiences. Children's PAA strategies were significantly associated with risks, emotion regulation and understanding, and symptoms. Children using highly coercive strategies showed the greatest difficulties. Emotion regulation and understanding also were associated with parent- and teacher-report of symptoms. These findings suggest that intervention efforts with at-risk youngsters should target only attachment security, but also emotional competence skills.

MARION. E. YOUNG (2009), Studied the aspects of emotional competence that protect people from stress, anxiety, and depression, and help to promote positive affect. A total of 163 university students completed a two wave study that involved measuring emotional competence and emotional well-being at 1-year intervals. As expected, Time 1 measures of emotional competence predicted Time 2 measures of well-being, after controlling for Time 1 measures of well-being. Specifically, ineffective problem orientation predicated increases in anxiety and stress, and decreases in positive affect. Difficulty identifying and describing emotions predicated increases in anxiety and decreases in positive affect. Finally, an aspect of difficulty managing emotions (i.e. rumination) predicated decreases in positive affect. Each emotional competence variable predicated unique variance after controlling for other significant variables.

DANIELLE M. HESSLER AND LYNN FAINSILBER KATZ (2009), examined associations between emotional competence (i.e., awareness, regulation, comfort with expression) and adolescent risky behavior. Children from a longitudinal study participated at age 9 and 16 (N=88). Semi-structured interviews were conducted with children about their emotional experiences and coded for areas of emotional competence. Associations were examined for the emotions of sadness and anger concurrently during adolescence, and longitudinally from middle childhood to adolescence. Results suggested that children with poor emotional awareness and regulation had a higher likelihood of using hard drugs. Findings suggest that children's emotional competence may serve as a useful point of intervention to decrease risky behavior in adolescence.

KUMAR (2009) conducted a study on mental health and emotional competence of prospective teachers of Himachal Pradesh in relation to their gender, stream and social category and found that male and female prospective teachers of science and arts streams belonging to open and reserved categories differed significantly in their "Adequate Depth of Feeling", "Adequate Expression and Control of Feeling", "Ability to Function with Emotions", "Ability to cope with problem Emotions" and "Encouragement of Positive Emotions" Component of emotional competence. Prospective teachers of science and arts streams belonging to open and reserved categories differed significantly in their total emotional competence.

PATRICIA AND MARK (2009) studied classroom teacher, social and emotional competence in relation to student and classroom out comes. The researchers proposed a model of the pro social classroom that highlights the importance of teachers" social and emotional competence (SEC) and well–being in the development and maintenance of supportive teacher–student relationships, effective classroom management and successful social and emotional learning programme implementation. This model proposes that these factors contribute to creating a classroom climate that is more conducive to learning and that promotes positive developmental outcomes among students. Furthermore, this article reviews current research suggesting a relationship between SEC and teacher burnout and reviews intervention efforts to support teachers" SEC through stress reduction and mindfulness programs. Finally, the authors propose a research agenda to address the potential efficacy of intervention.

RANA (2011) found that level of emotional competence and other variables i.e. sex, stream, family type and type of school did not interact significantly with respect to their combined influence on aggression among senior secondary school students.

NAVEEN.K (2011) examined "the emotional competence level of teacher educators". This study aimed at finding the emotional competence level of teacher educators working in B.Ed. colleges with respect to their gender, experience, educational level and marital status. The study was carried out on a sample of 150 teacher educators of district Sonepat and Panipat of

Haryana State. The results revealed that teacher educators have an average level of emotional competence and there is no significant difference in the level of emotional competence of teacher educators with respect to their gender, experience, educational level and marital status

COLLE, L. AND DEL GIUDICE, M. (2011), investigated the relationship between patterns of attachment and emotional competence at the beginning of middle childhood in a sample of 122 seven-year-olds. A new battery of tasks was developed in order to asses two facets of emotional competence (emotion recognition and knowledge of regulation strategies). Attachment was related to the choice of emotion regulation strategies in hypothetical situations.

BAGHERI (2012) investigated the emotional competence and self-esteem in students of performing arts and students of other fields of art. The results showed that there was significant difference between performing artists and non-performing artists in emotional competence. Emotional competence level of performing artists was significantly higher than the non-performing artists.

BAKSHI (2012) conducted a study on emotional competence of adolescents in relation to cognitive and non-cognitive variables and found a positive correlation of emotional competence with intelligence, creativity, academic achievement, family environment and mental health.

KATNA (2012) found no significant difference in the emotional competence of senior secondary school students in relation to their gender, stream, locality, type of school and social category.

KUMAR (2012) found that secondary school students having competent, average and incompetent level of emotional competence possessed the same level of aggressive behaviour. Also the emotional competence level and gender, stream, and institution type did not interact significantly with regard to their combined influence on aggression among students.

SUNIL KUMAR (2012) studied on "Emotional competence of senior secondary school teachers in relation to their age, gender, type of school & locality "In developing society, a teacher has assumed a greater responsibility to bring out good citizens who could carry out the profession in a dignified and productive manner. To support the work of the organization teachers must have not only technical management skill but also skill in managing emotions, there as well as those of other individuals in the organization. Emotional competent teacher exhibits a high regard for colleagues and subordinates, an understanding of basic motivations as well as basic justice, as willingness to correct faculty situations, and a willingness to take positive, quick, and aggressive action when indicated. In this context the investigators conducted a study of Emotional Competence of 200 senior secondary school teachers. The major objectives of the study were to compare the Emotional Competence of male and female, rural and urban teachers. The Emotional Competence Scale (ECS) by H.C. Sharma and R. Bharadwaj was used to assess the effectiveness of teachers. Mean, S.D and't' test were used to analyze the data. The results indicated that no significant difference was found in Emotional Competence of teachers on the basis of gender whereas a significant difference has been found in Emotional Competence of teachers on the basis of their age and type of school.

SHARMA AND SUMAN LATA (2013) studied on "Comparative Study of Emotional Competence among students in relation to their Gender and Type of Institute" The major objective of the investigation was to compare the emotional competence among students studying in K.V (KendriyaVidyalaya) and Non K.V schools. It was hypothesized that no significant difference of emotional competence among students studying in K.V and non K.V schools. For verification of the hypothesis, the data was collected by administering 'Emotional competence scale' on 200 students of Ludhiana district of Punjab by adopting convenient sampling technique. Mean, SD and t-ratio was used for analyzing data. The finding of the present study revealed that emotional competence of K.V students significantly differ from non K.V students. There is no significant difference in emotional competence of Non KV boys and Non KV girl students of Ludhiana Dist. Another finding of present indicates that gender does not affect emotional competence.

SHARMA RITU (2013) examined "A Study of Emotional Competence of Visually Impaired Adolescents" The study was conducted on Visually Impaired Adolescents to know their emotional competence. For the purpose, Scale of Emotional Competence (Sharma H.C. and Bhardwaj, R.) was administered to a sample of 18 visually impaired adolescents (12 boys and 6 girls). Results showed that both genders possess average level of emotional competence. It was seen that only in one component of emotional competence (encouragement of positive emotions) females scored than males.

STUDIES RELATED TO LEADERSPIP PREFERENCE

STOGDILL (1948) summarized his research on Leadership by analyzing some124 bibliographical items. The average person who occupies a position of leadership exceeds the average member of his group in the following respects: Intelligence, scholarship, dependability in exercising responsibilities, activity and social participation and socio- economic status. The average person who occupies a position of leadership exceeds the average members of his group to some degree in the following respects: sociability, initiatives, persistence, knowing how to get things done, self- confidence, alertness, and insight into situations, cooperativeness, popularity, adaptability, and verbal facility.

FIELDLER (1967) developed what he called a contingency model of leadership effectiveness. This model contained the relationship between leadership style and the favorableness of the situation. Situational favorableness was described by Fielders in terms of three empirically derived dimensions. The leader member relationship, which is the most critical variable in determining the situations favorableness. The degree of task structure is considered to be the second most important input into the favorableness of the situation. The leaders position, power obtained through formal authority is the third most critical dimension of the situation. Situations are favorable if all three of the above dimensions are high. If the leader is generally accepted by the followers, if the task is very structured and everything is spelled out and if the great deal of authority and power is formally attributed to the leaders position. Then the situation is favorable to the leader. Fieldler was convinced that the favorableness of the situation in combination with the leadership style determine effectiveness.

BHUSHAN (1968) explored the relationship between personality variables and preference for in authoritarian or democratic leadership. A random sample of 400 undergraduate male students belonging to middle and lower middle income groups of families was drawn from constituent college of Bhagalpur university.

- Personality factors were substantially related to the leadership preference
- Preference for a democratic type of leadership was negative related to authoritarianism.
- Personality factors exerted a direct influence upon individual choice of as authoritarian as democratic leadership and were significantly higher.
- Factors like residence in rural or urban areas, age, stay in the college and financial status did not have any significant influence on to the leadership preference.

SHARMA (1986) conducted a comparative study on 150NSS leaders drawn from three male colleges and female colleges, affiliated to the Meerut University to find out the leadership effectiveness. The magnitude to which personality traits contributed to the leadership effectiveness and personality traits of the student leaders. The major findings were the following, Personality traits contributed to leadership effectiveness but not to an appreciable degree. The leadership trait was contingent on distinctive growth levels of different personality traits. Leadership as a trait was found to develop only in a very small section of population.

SAXENA (1987) conducted a development study on 200 student leaders to find out the personality characteristics of student leaders at higher secondary level. The developmental trends includes frustrations among student leaders. The major findings were the following:

- Leaders process very limited personality dispositions like were out going, emotionally stable, excitable venturesome, tough-minded, vigorous and confident.
- In this attitude to parents the higher secondary students did not differ significantly from non-leaders.

BAN ENG GOH (1991) has investigated a study on cross cultural study of leadership, social maturity and creative potential in adolescents. The study investigated the relationship among adolescents in United States and Singapore. Results showed higher intelligence but lower leadership potential among Singapore students and positive correlation in general between social maturity and intelligence, while creativity was found to be negatively correlated with both intelligence and academic achievement.

BRUCE (1991) examined children's leadership expression in different types of group activities form early elementary school through high school. Parents and teachers of 354 students from kindergarten to twelfth grade public school in Western New York completed questionnaires assessing their children's leadership expression. Findings indicated that Leadership in social activities outside the family was greater for High school students than for younger students, while leadership in family activities was less. Female students were more involved in social activities than compared to male students.

RANEEY DAVID. A (1991) investigated research in the field of management leadership development and human development. The research suggests that the equality of as individual's personal life, the effectiveness of his/her professional.

Manu (1992) conducted a survey to identify the leadership potentials and non-potentials and to study the nature of interests and styles associated with potential and no potentials

- A significantly high correlation was obtained between cognitive style and leadership potential scores.
- Interest and cognitive style together were good predicators of leadership potential leaders were warm, emotionally stable, assertive, enthusiastic, conscientious, adventurous and controlled.
- Potential and non-potential leaders were obedient sober, indifferent to rules shy and uncontrolled.

BUCKNER (1995) made an attempt to measure university student leaders' leadership roles. 76 student leaders answered a questionnaire. Buckner used a theoretical model of organizational effectiveness and leadership, developed by Robert Quinn in 1988, which was adapted and applied to student leadership programs. Overall results of the study indicated that: student leaders saw themselves most often as mentors to others within their organization or club. Student leaders saw themselves least often as brokers to individuals outside their immediate units. Position of leadership, type of organization or club, student classification and gender produced significant differences in the leadership roles performed.

RUSCH (1995) presented the findings of a study that located the underlying values that support the social construction of democratic practice in schools. It explored how school leaders in democratic school communities viewed the dialectic relationship between schools and communities and between democratic beliefs and practices, identified the underlying factors that loster the democratic practices understand leadership as an idea, but not as a process. They exhibit equity in their language and behavior. They view "learning together" as school culture. They engage in building capacity to relate democratic leaders.

Pavitt, Charles et al (1995) Investigated on participation of leadership held by young females 50 participants in a Mississippi leadership program were female high school juniors and seniors who reported that family members provided the greatest influence, student government provided the greatest opportunities and shyness was the biggest obstacle. They did not believe that popularity was prerequisite to leadership or that males make better leaders.

PAVITT, CHARLES ET AL (1995) Investigated on the objective and subjective sides of leadership communications and social judgment in decision making groups, they found judgment of communicative behaviors strongly predicated leadership evaluation but measures of actual communications were poor predictors of trait judgment and leadership evaluations and were generally unrelated with judgments of these behavior.

LASHWAY (1997) Synthesizing the research in leaders' behavior distinguishes between style and strategy. Style is a reflection of personal makeup a set of predispositions that people bring to the job. Strategy is a consciously chosen pattern of behavior designed to gain the cooperation of followers in accomplishing organizational goals, strategies develop from the way leaders view power as well as form what they notice when they analyze a situation.

CONCLUSION

Survey of related studies consist of searching, identifying and evaluating report of relevant research, which is valuable in formulating and studying the problem; it previous pointless repetition of research. Above all, it contributes to the general scholarship of the investigation.

❐

13

Design and Method of Investigation

This chapter gives us over all view of the design of the study, research tools used in the study, nature and selection of the sample and a brief description of the procedure adapted for collection of data. This chapter also includes the view of reliability and validity of the variables used for the study.

HYPOTHESES OF THE STUDY

The hypotheses framed in the present study are listed below:

1. The level of Emotional competence of high school students is average in nature.
2. The level of Leadership preference of high school students is average in nature.
3. There is no significant difference between the mean scores of Emotional competence of high school students with regard to

Gender	:	Male / Female
Type of management	:	Govt / Govt aided / Private
Birth order	:	First born/ Middle born / Last born
Type of family	:	Joint / Nuclear

4. There is no significant difference between the mean scores of Leadership preference of high school students.
    - Gender
    - Type of management
    - Birth order
    - Type of family
5. There is no significant correlation between the Emotional competence and Leadership preference of high school students.

TOOLS AND TECHNIQUES USED

The following tools have been used in the present study.

1. Emotional competence Assessment Scale (ECAS) inventory prepared by Suresh kumar. M and Fulton Paiva. J.S. (2009)
2. Leadership preference inventory by L.I. Bhushan.
3. Emotional competenceAssessment Scale

Description

This scale is constructed and validated by the Suresh kumar. M and FultonPaiva. J.S. It consists of 35 items in which each item has two statements.

Administration

Students were asked to sit comfortably and fill their general data on the data sheet given. Even though there was no time limit to finish the questionnaire, students completed the task within 20 minutes. They were also told that their responses would be kept confidential and used strictly on the purpose of research only.

Scoring

All the statements are rated by four point scale. Always (3 points), sometimes (2 points), rarely (1 point) and Never (0 point) . For measuring Emotional Competence, total responses marks were taken by the investigator according to their choices.

LEADERSHIP PREFERENCE INVENTORY

Description

It is constructed and validated by the L.I. Bhushan. It consists of 30 items in which each item has two statements.

Administration

Students were asked to sit comfortably and fill their general data on the data sheet given. Even though there was no time limit to finish the questionnaire, students completed the task within 15 minutes. They were also told that their responses would be kept confidential and used strictly on the purpose of research only.

Scoring

The entire item the test indicates the preference.

TABLE.13.1: Showing the Nature of Statements in the Leadership Preference Scale

Leadership preference	Item Number	Marks				
		Fully disagree	Disagree	Uncertain	Agree	Fully agree
	1,2,3,5,8,12,13,14,16,18, 20,22,23,24,27.	1	2	3	4	5
	4,6,7,9,10,11,15,17,19, 21,25,26,28,29,30	5	4	3	2	1

Sample

A good sample of a population is the one which within restrictions imposed by its size, will reproduce the characteristics of the population with the greatest possible accuracy (**S.O. Sukhia**, 1963). The present study is mainly concerned with 300 students studying in the high Schools in Government, Government aided and private schools in Vellore District, Tamil Nadu.

TABLE.13.2: Showing the Details of the Composition of the Sample

Type of schools	Name of School	Number of students selected		
		Boys	**Girls**	**Total**
Government	Govt Municipal High School	34	48	82
Government Aided	CSI Goodlet Hr. Sec School	62	37	99
Private	Holy cross Matric Hr. Sec. School	67	52	119
	Total	**163**	**137**	**300**

PILOT STUDY

Before finalizing the final form of the tools and collecting data for main study, a pilot study was attempted in October 2014. It was conducted on 50 eleventh standard students drawing from each school selected randomly from the whole sample to establish reliability and validity of the various tools used in the study.

ESTABLISHING RELIABILITY AND VALIDITY

The reliability of a test may be defined as the degree of consistency with which the test measures what it does measures. A test score is called reliable, when we have reasons to believe it to be stable and trustworthy.

Emotional Competence scale

Reliability

In order to establish the reliability of the Emotional competence assessment scale, the split half method was used and it was found to be 0.71. Hence Emotional Competence Assessment Scale is considered as a reliable tool.

Validity

The validity of this tool was found out by computing the square root of the reliability co efficient which worked out to be 0.84. Hence this tool is highly valid.

Leadership preference Inventory

Reliability

To find out the reliability of the leadership preference scale, split half method was used and the reliability of co-efficient was found to be 0.79 which suggest that the tool is reliable.

Validity

The validity of this tool was also found out by the same way and it was 0.88. Hence this tool is highly valid.

MAIN STUDY

The validated tools were made use for the main study to collect the necessary data in November 2014. The time schedule for each of these tests finalized on the basis of the pilot study.

TABLE.13.3: Showing the Time Schedule of Administered Tools

S. No.	Name of test	Time Taken (Minutes)
1.	Emotional competence inventory	20
2.	Leadership preference inventory	15
	Total	**35**

STATISTICAL TECHNIQUES USED

Suitable descriptive and inferential statistical techniques were used in the interpretation of the data to draw out a more meaningful picture of results from the collected data. In the present study, the following statistical measures were used.

1. Mean

$$\bar{X} = A + \frac{\sum fd}{\sum f} \times i$$

Where

A = Assumed mean

f = frequency

d = deviation from the assumed mean

i = class interval

2. Standard Deviation

$$SD(\sigma) = \sqrt{\frac{\sum fd^2}{N} - \left[\frac{\sum fd^2}{N}\right]^2} \times i$$

where

f = frequency

i = class interval

N = Total frequency

d = Deviation from arithmetic mean

3. Standard Error Deviation

$$\text{SED} = \sqrt{\frac{\sigma_1^2}{N_1} + \frac{\sigma_2^2}{N_2}}$$

Where

M_1, M_2 = Standard deviation

$N_1\ N_2$ = Total number of sample

4. t-Test

To compute the significance of difference between mean of various measures, t-test was used. 't' ratio was calculated from the relation.

$$\text{t-value} = \frac{M_1 \sim M_2}{\sqrt{\frac{\sigma_1^2}{N_1} + \frac{\sigma_1^2}{N_2}}} = \frac{M_1 \sim M_2}{S \in D}$$

Where

$M_1\ M_2$ = Mean of the groups

$\sigma_1\ \sigma_2$ = Standard -Deviations

$N_1\ N_2$ = Total number of sample

5. Correlation Co-efficient

$$r = \frac{N\sum x \sum y - \sum x \sum y}{\sqrt{\left(N\sum x^2 - \left(\sum x^2\right)\right)\left(N\sum Y^2 - \left(\sum y\right)^2\right.}}$$

where

X, Y = Variables

N = Total strength

6. Chi-Square Distribution

$$x^2 = \sum \frac{(fo - fe)^2}{fe}$$

Where f_o = Observed frequency

f_e = Expected frequency

7. F-Test

$$C = \frac{\left(\sum x_1 + \sum x_2 + \sum x_3\right)^2}{N}$$

$$TSS = \sum x_1^2 + \sum x_2^2 + \sum x_3^2 - C$$

$$BSS = \frac{\left(\sum x_1\right)^2}{n_1} + \frac{\left(\sum x_2\right)^2}{n_2} + \frac{\left(\sum x_3\right)}{n_3} - C$$

$$WSS = TSS - BSS$$

$$t_1 = \frac{BSS}{dfB}; t_2 = \frac{WSS}{dfW}$$

$$F = \frac{t_1}{t_2}$$

Where C = Correction term

$\sum X_1, \sum X_2, \sum X_3,$ = Sum of the scores of each groups.

N = Total number of Sample

n_1, n_2, n_3 = Number of sample of each groups

TSS = Total Number of Squares

BSS = Sum of squares between the group means

WSS = Sum of squares within the group

dfB = Degrees of freedom for the between group means.

dfw = Degrees of freedom for within group means

t_1 = Mean sum of squares between the group

t_2 = Mean sum of squares within the group.

CONCLUSION

This chapter outlines the design of the present study, the procedure followed and the nature of the sample. It describes the hypotheses to be tested, the tools used and methods of administration and scoring. Adopting the methods and procedures discussed earlier in this chapter, tests were administered and marked. The obtained data were then analyzed, using appropriate statistical techniques described above to study the effect of Emotional competence and Leadership preference, the results of which are discussed in the light of hypotheses formulated and the next chapter presents this analysis and discussion part of the study.

❐

14

Analysis and Interpretation of Data

The result section describes the statistical techniques or the inferential interpretations that were applied to the data, and the results of these analyses. For each hypothesis, the statistical test of significance selected and applied to the data is described, followed by a statement indicating whether the hypothesis was supported or non-supported. Tables present the numerical data are uncluttered and self-explanatory. Charts and diagrams showing the relationships among identified topics, categories and patterns are presented in the result section.

The logic and description of the interpretation linked to qualitative charts and diagrams is an important aspect of qualitative research.

CLASSIFICATION OF THE SAMPLE BASED ON THE VARIABLES OF THE STUDY

EMOTIONAL COMPETENCE

Hypothesis-1

The level of Emotional Competence among the High School Students is Average in nature.

TABLE.14.01: Showing the level of Emotional Competence among the High School Students

Variable	Number of sample	Level	No. of Students	Percentage %
Emotional Competence	300	Low	77	26.3
		Average	139	46.0
		High	84	27.7

INFERENCE

From the above table it is inferred that the level of Emotional Competence among the High School Students is Moderate in nature.

Hence, the Hypothesis-1 is accepted.

LEADERSHIP PREFERENCE

Hypothesis-2

The level of Leadership Preference among High School Students is average in nature.

TABLE .14.2: Showing the level of Leadership Preference among High School Students.

Variable	Number of Sample	Level	No. of Students	Percentage
Leadership Preference	300	Low	75	25.0
		Average	143	47.7
		High	82	27.3

INFERENCE

From the above table it is inferred that the level of Leadership Preference among the High School Students is average in nature.

Hence, the hypothesis – 2 is accepted.

EMOTIONAL COMPETENCE

INFLUENCE OF GENDER ON EMOTIONAL COMPETENCE

Hypothesis-3

There is no significant difference between the Mean Scores of Emotional Competence of High School Students with regard to Gender.

TABLE.14.3: Showing the significant difference of High School Students' Emotional Competence based on Gender

Variable	Gender	Number of Samples	Mean	Standard Deviation	Critical ratio	Level of Significance
Emotional Competence	Boys	113	72.42	12.157	4.848	0.01
	Girls	187	80.09	13.901		

INFERENCE

From the above table, it is observed that the obtained critical ratio value (4.848) is higher than the table value (2.58) at 0.01 level. So there is significant difference in High School Students' Emotional Competence based on gender. **Hence the null hypothesis – 3 is rejected.**

INFLUENCE OF TYPE OF MANAGEMENT ON EMOTIONAL COMPETENCE

Hypothesis-4

There is no significant difference between the Mean Scores of Emotional Competence of High School Students with regard to Type of Management.

TABLE .14.4: ANOVA – Showing the Emotional Competence of High School Students based on Type of Management.

Variable	Sources of Variation	Sum of Squares	Degrees of Freedom	Mean Squares	F-value	LS
Emotional Competence	Between groups	11548.242	2	5774.121	38.336	0.01
	Within groups	45086.355	297	151.806		
	Total	**56634.597**	**299**			

INFERENCE

From the above table it is clear that the calculated F- value (38.336) is greater than the table value (4.71) at (0.01) level. Therefore further analysis can be done to find out the significant difference between the three groups.

TABLE.14.5: Showing the Significant Difference between the mean Scores of High School Students' Emotional Competency based on Type of Management

Variable	Gender	Number	Mean	Standard Deviation	Critical Ratio	Level of Significance
Emotional competence	Government Vs Govt-Aided	83	73.19	10.394	0.873	NS
		102	71.64	13.215		
	Govt-Aided Vs Private	102	71.64	13.251	7.588	0.01
		115	85.03	12.736		
	Private Vs Government	115	85.03	12.736	6.960	0.01
		83	73.19	10.394		

From the above table it is clear that the obtained critical ratio value (0.873) is lesser than the table value (1.96). So, there is no significant difference between government and government aided High School Students' based on emotional competency.

In the 2nd case, it is clear that the obtained critical ratio value (7.588) is greater than the table value (2.58) at (0.01) level. So, there is significant difference between government aided and private High School Students' based on emotional competency. Here, private High School Students have more emotional competency than government aided High School Students.

In the 3rd case it is clear that the obtained critical ratio value (6.960) is greater than the table value (2.58) at (0.01) level. So, there is significant difference between private and government High School Students' based on emotional competency.

Therefore Private High School Students have more emotional competency than the Government and Government-Aided Students. **Hence the null hypothesis – 4 is partially verified.**

INFLUENCE OF BIRTH ORDER ON EMOTIONAL COMPETENCY

Hypothesis-5

There is no significant difference between the mean scores of Emotional Competence of high school students with regard to Birth order.

TABLE.14.6: ANOVA – Showing the Emotional Competence of High School Students based on their Birth Order

Variable	Sources of Variation	Sum of Squares	Degrees of Freedom	Mean Squares	F-Value	LS
Emotional Competence	Between groups	758.547	2	379.135	2.016	**NS**
	Within groups	55876.050	297	188.135		
	Total	**56634.597**	**299**			

INFERENCE

From the above table it is clear that the calculated F- value (2.016) is lesser than the table value (3.04). Hence it shows that there is no significant difference in High School Students' emotional competency based on their birth order. **Hence, the null hypothesis – 5 is accepted.**

INFLUENCE OF TYPE OF FAMILY ON EMOTIONAL COMPETENCE

Hypothesis-6

There is no significant difference between the mean scores of Emotional Competence of high school students with regard to Type of Family.

TABLE.14.7: Showing the Significant Difference of High School Students' Emotional Competence based on Type of Family

Variable	Type of Family	Number of Samples	Mean	Standard Deviation	Critical Ratio	Level of Significance
Emotional Competence	Nuclear	201	77.06	13.552	0.257	**NS**
	Joint	99	77.49	14.247		

INFERENCE

From the above table it is clear that the obtained critical ratio value (.257) is lesser than the table value (1.96). So, there is no significant difference between nuclear and joint family of High School Students' Emotional Competency. **Hence, the null hypothesis -6 is accepted.**

LEADERSHIP PREFERENCE

INFLUENCE OF GENDER ON LEADERSHIP PREFERENCE

Hypothesis-7

There is no significant difference between the Mean Scores of leadership preference of High School Students with regard to Gender.

TABLE.14.8: Showing the Mean, Standard Deviation and Critical Ratio of High School Students' Leadership Preference based on Gender

Variable	Gender	Number of Samples	Mean	Standard Deviation	Critical Ratio	Level of Significance
Leadership Preference	Boys	113	102.72	10.399	4.015	**0.01**
	Girls	187	108.31	12.405		

INFERENCE

From the above table it is clear that the obtained Critical Ratio Value (4.015) is greater than the table value (2.58) at (0.01) level. So, there is significant difference in High School Students' Leadership Preference based on Gender. **Hence, the null hypothesis -7 is rejected.**

INFLUENCE OF TYPE OF MANAGEMENT ON LEADERSHIP PREFERENCE

Hypothesis-8

There is no significant difference between the Mean Scores of leadership preference of high school students with regard to Type of Management.

TABLE.14.9: ANOVA – Showing the Leadership Preference of High School Students based on Type of Management

Variable	Sources of Variation	Sum of Squares	Degrees of Freedom	Mean Squares	F-Value	LS
Emotional Competence	Between groups	2468.983	2	1234.492	9.060	0.01
	Within groups	40467.613	297	136.255		
	Total	**42936.597**	**299**			

INFERENCE

From the above table it is clear that the calculated F- value (9.060) is greater than the table value (4.66) at (0.01) level. Therefore further analysis can be done to find out the significance difference between the three groups.

TABLE.14.10: Showing the Significant Difference between the Mean scores of High School Students' Leadership Preference based on Type of Management.

Variable	Gender	Number	Mean	Standard Deviation	Critical Ratio	Level of significance
Leadership Preference	Government Vs Govt-Aided	83	110.22	7.948	5.308	0.01
		102	102.87	10.366		
	Govt-Aided Vs Private	102	102.87	10.366	1.945	NS
		115	106.26	14.640		
	Private Vs Government	115	106.26	14.640	2.235	0.05
		83	110.22	7.948		

From the above table it is clear that the obtained Critical Ratio Value (5.308) is greater than the table value (2.58) at (0.01) level. So, there is significant difference between Government and Government aided High School Students' Leadership Preference.

In the 2nd case, it is clear that the obtained critical ratio value (1.945) is lesser than the table value (1.96) at (0.05) level. So, there is no significant difference between government aided and private High School Students' Leadership Preference.

In the 3rd case, it is clear that the obtained critical ratio value (2.235) is greater than the table value (1.96) at (0.05) level. So, there is significant difference between Private and Government High School Students' Leadership Preference.

Therefore government school students have more leadership preference than the government aided and private school students. **Hence the null hypothesis –9 is partially verified.**

INFLUENCE OF BIRTH ORDER ON LEADERSHIP PREFERENCE

Hypothesis-9

There is no significant difference between the Mean Scores of Emotional Competence of high school students with regard to Birth order.

TABLE.14.11: ANOVA – Showing the Leadership Preference of High School Students based on Birth Order

Variable	Sources of Variation	Sum of Squares	Degrees of Freedom	Mean Squares	F-Value	LS
Emotional Competence	Between groups	1218.548	2	609.274	4.338	0.05
	Within groups	41718.049	297	140.465		
	Total	42936.597	299			

INFERENCE

From the above table it is clear that the calculated F- value (4.338) is greater than the table value (3.02) at (0.05) level. Therefore further analysis can be done to find out the significance difference between the three groups.

TABLE.14.12: Showing the Significant Difference in a Mean Score of High School Students' Leadership Preference based on their Birth Order

Variable	Order of Birth	Number	Mean	Standard Deviation	Critical Ratio	Level of Significance
Leadership preference	First born Vs Middle born	131	104.35	13.416	2.646	0.01
		51	110.04	11.948		
	Middle born Vs Last born	51	110.04	11.948	1.958	NS
		118	106.60	9.776		
	Last born Vs First born	118	106.60	9.776	1.499	NS
		131	104.35	13.416		

From the above table it is clear that the obtained critical ratio value (2.646) is greater than the table value (2.58) at (0.01) level. So, there is significant difference between First and Middle Born High School Students' Leadership Preference.

In the 2nd case it is clear that the obtained Critical Ratio Value (1.958) is lesser than the table value (1.96) at (0.05) level. So, there is no significant difference between Middle and Last Born High School Students' Leadership Preference.

In the 3rd case it is clear that the obtained Critical Ratio Value (1.499) is lesser than the table value (1.96) at (0.05) level. So, there is no significant difference between Last and First Born High School Students' Leadership Preference.

Therefore middle born high school students have more leadership preference than the first born and last born high school students. **Hence the null hypothesis- 10 is partially verified.**

INFLUENCE OF TYPE OF FAMILY ON LEADERSHIP PREFERENCE

Hypothesis-10

There is no significant difference between the Mean Scores of Emotional Competence of High School Students with regard to Type of Family.

TABLE.14.13: Showing the Mean, Standard Deviation and Critical Ratio of High School Students' Leadership Preference based on Type of Family

Variable	Type of Family	Number of Samples	Mean	Standard Deviation	Critical Ratio	Level of Significance
Leadership Preference	Nuclear	201	107.10	12.430	1 864	NS
	Joint	99	104.37	10.852		

INFERENCE

From the above table it is clear that the obtained Critical Ratio Value (1.864) is lesser than the table value (1.96) at (0.05) level. So, there is no significant difference between Nuclear and Joint Family High School Students' leadership preference. **Hence, the null hypothesis -10 is accepted.**

CORRELATION BETWEEN EMOTIONAL COMPETENCE AND LEADERSHIP PREFERENCE

Hypothesis-11

There is no significant correlation between the Emotional Competence and Leadership Preference of High School Students.

TABLE.14.14: Showing the Correlation between Emotional Competence and Leadership Preference of High School Students

Comparison of Variable	Sample Size	Correlation	Level of Significance
Emotional Competence Vs Leadership Preference	300	0.142	0.05

INFERENCE

From the above table, it is clearly observed that there is significant correlation between Emotional Competence and Leadership Preference among high school students

Therefore, the null hypothesis is rejected.

CONCLUSION

The analysis and interpretation of data represent the application of deductive and inductive logic to the research process. The data are often classified by division into subgroups and then analyzed and synthesized in such a way that hypothesis may be verified or rejected. The final results may be a new principle of generalization, like interpretation of results, the formulation of conclusion and generalization also demand s key dissertations. Wide outlook in depth knowledge and power of logical thinking, a brief report of the present research study together with major findings and conclusion have been presented in the succeeding chapter.

❐

15

Summary, Findings and Conclusion

This chapter deals with the consolidation of the various findings presented in the previous chapter. Findings are statement of factual information based upon the data analysis. Conclusion is answers to the question raised or the statements of acceptance or rejection of the hypotheses proposed. In this chapter the researcher deals with the aspects pertaining to the tools used for the investigation, objectives and hypotheses of study, based on analysis the major findings arrived at, all finally the educational implication together with suggestion for further study. The aim of the present investigations is to study the Emotional competence on Leadership preference among high secondary school students.

STATEMENT OF THE PROBLEM

The present study is entitled as, ***"Influence of Emotional competence on Leadership preference among high school students".***

OBJECTIVES OF THE STUDY

The objectives framed in the present study are listed below:

1. To find out the level of Emotional Competence of high school students.

2. To find out the level of Leadership Preference of high school students.
3. To find out whether there is any significant difference between the mean scores of Emotional competence of high school students.

Gender	:	Male / Female
Type of management	:	Govt /Govt aided/ Private
Birth order	:	First born/Middle born /Last born
Type of family	:	Nuclear/ joint

4. To find out whether there is any significant difference between the mean scores of Leadership preference of high school students.
   - Gender
   - Type of management
   - Birth order
   - Type of family
5. To find out whether there is any significant correlation between the Emotional competence and Leadership preference of high school students.

HYPOTHESES OF THE STUDY

The hypotheses framed in the present study are listed below:

1. The level of Emotional competence of high school students is average in nature.
2. The level of Leadership preference of high school students is average in nature.
3. There is no significant difference between the Emotional competences of high school students.

Gender	:	Boys / Girls
Type of management	:	Govt / Govt. Aided / Private
Birth order	:	First Born / Middle Born / Last Born
Type of family	:	Nuclear / Joint

4. There is no significant difference between the mean scores of Leadership preference of high school students.
   - Gender
   - Type of management
   - Birth order
   - Type of family
5. There is no significant correlation between the Emotional competence and Leadership preference of high school students.

SAMPLE OF THE STUDY

A stratified random sampling technique was adapted for the selection of sample. The schools selected for this study are divided into different strata: Government, Government Aided and Private schools. The random sampling technique was adopted to select the sample. Data were collected from 300 students, 82 students were drawn from government school, 99 from government aided school and 119 from private school. The students studying in standard IX in the schools of Chennai city were chosen as sample.

TOOLS AND TECHNIQUES USED

The following tools have been used in the present study.

- Emotional Competence Assessment Scale (ECAS) inventory prepared by Suresh kumar. M and Fulton Pavia. J.S. (2009).
- Leadership preference prepared by L.I. Bhushan.

MAJOR FINDINGS

1. The level of Emotional Competence among High School Students is Average in nature.
2. The level of Leadership Preference among High School Students is average in nature.
3. There is significant difference in High School Students' Emotional Competence based on gender.
4. Private High School Students have more emotional competency than the government and government aided and High School Students.
5. There is no significant difference in High School Students' emotional competency based on their birth order.
6. There is no significant difference between nuclear and joint family of High School Students' Emotional Competency.
7. There is significant difference in High School Students' Leadership Preference based on Gender.
8. Government school students have more leadership preference Govt. aided and private school students.
9. Middle born high school students have more leadership preference than the first born and last born high school students.
10. There is no significant difference between Nuclear and Joint Family High School Students' leadership preference.

EDUCATIONAL IMPLICATIONS

For emotional competence to have relevance for education, students need to be educated to become knowledgeable, responsible and able to deal effectively with their emotions and schools must work to meet the challenge by offering more than the basic teaching in the traditional academic areas.

Schools have to adopt comprehensive school based programs within the curriculum to promote students' social and emotional competence, enhance students' academic success, healthy growth and development, ability to maintain positive relationship and motivation to contribute to their communities.

Strong accountable leadership has always been a hall mark of successful school. The educational leader most strive to improve human condition through reflective study of human development, learning and diversity employ appropriate curricular decisions. They themselves able to establish mutual rest respect and a certain warmth and rapport with members of their group will be more effective.

Thus emotional competence and leadership preference are very much important for the student community.

SUGGESTIONS FOR FURTHER RESEARCH

1. A study may be conducted to college students studying in different areas of Tamil Nadu.
2. A comparative study may be undertaken to study and compare emotional competence and leadership preference of teaching professionals with other technical professionals like MBBS, Engineering etc. of Tamil Nadu.
3. The present study is limited to schools in Vellore district. It could be extended to other schools at Tamil Nadu state.

CONCLUSION

The purpose of the present investigation is to investigate the influence of Emotional Competence of leadership preference of high school students. The investigation is sure to find some usefulness in the field of education and findings of the investigation can serve a database for further research.

❐

Bibliography

1. Fry (Eds.), The human quest for meaning (pp. 27-50). Mahwah, NJ: ErlbaumMaddi, S. R. (1967). The existential neurosis. Journal of Abnormal Psychology, 72, 311-325.
2. Fry, P. S. (2000). Religious involvement, spirituality and personal meaning for life: Existential predictors of psychological wellbeing in community-residing and institutional care elders. Aging and Mental Health, 4, 375-387.
3. Gardner, H. (1983). Frames of mind. The theory of multiple intelligences. New York: Basic Books.
4. Gardner, H. (2000). A case against spiritual intelligence. The Internat-ional Journal for the Psychology of Religion, 10, 27-34.
5. Halama, P., &Strizenec, M. (2004). Spiritual, existential or both? Theoret-ical con-siderations on the nature of higher intelligences. StudiaPsychologica, 43, 239-253
6. Hewitt, P. L., &Flett, G. L. (1991). Perfectionism in the self and social contexts:
7. Conceptualization, assessment, and association with psychopathology. *Journal of Personality and Social Psychology,* 60, 456–470.
8. Hewitt, P. L., &Flett, G. L. (1991). Perfectionism in the self and social contexts: Conceptualization, assessment, and association with psychopathology. *Journal of Personality and Social Psychology,* 60, 456–470.
9. Hewitt, P. L., &Flett, G. L. (2004). *Multidimensional Perfectionism Scale (MPS): Technical manual.* Toronto, Canada: Multi-Health Systems.

10. Hewitt, P. L., & Flett, G. L. (2004). *Multidimensional Perfectionism Scale (MPS): Technical manual.* Toronto, Canada: Multi-Health Systems.
11. Klinger, E. (1998). The search for meaning in evolutionary perspective and its clinical implications. In P. T. P. Wong & P. S.
12. Kutner, M. H., Nachtsheim, C. J., &Neter, J. (2004). *Applied linear regression models* (4th ed.). New York: McGraw-Hill.
13. Kutner, M. H., Nachtsheim, C. J., & Neter, J. (2004). *Applied linear regression models* (4th ed.). New York: McGraw-Hill.
14. MacDonald, D.A. and Holland, D. (2003). Spirituality and the MMPI-2. Journal of Clinical Psychology, 59(4): 399–410.
15. Machovec, F. J. (2002). Spiritual intelligence: Behavioral sciences and the humanities. Lewiston, N.Y.: Edwin Mullen Press.
16. Maehr, M. L., &Zusho, A. (2009). Achievement goal theory: The past, present, and future. In K. R. Wentzel& A. Wigfield (Eds.), *Handbook of motivation in school* (pp. 77–104). New York: Taylor & Francis.
17. Maehr, M. L., &Zusho, A. (2009). Achievement goal theory: The past, present, and future. In K. R. Wentzel& A. Wigfield (Eds.), *Handbook of motivation in school* (pp. 77–104). New York: Taylor & Francis.
18. Mascaro, N., & Rosen, D. H. (2005). Existential meaning's role in the enhancement of hope and prevention of depressive symptoms. Journal of Personality, 73, 985-1014.
19. Mascaro, N., & Rosen, D. H. (2006). The role of existential meaning as a buffer against stress. Journal of Humanistic Psychology, 46, 168-190.
20. Maslow, A. H. (1964). Religions, values, and peak-experiences. Arkana: Penguin Books.
21. Mayer, J. (2000). Spiritual intelligence or spiritual consciousness? The International Journal for the Psychology of Religion, 10, 47–56.
22. Mayer, J. D. (2000). Spiritual intelligence or spiritual consciousness? The International Journal for the Psychology of Religion, 10, 47-56.
23. Mayer, J. D., Caruso, D., &Salovey, P. (2000). Emotional intelligence meets traditional standards for an intelligence. Intelligence, 27, 267-298
24. McCall, G. J., & Simmons, J. L. (1966). Identities and interactions: An examination of human associations in everyday life. New York: Free Press.
25. McCrae, Robert R., and Paul T. Costa. (2003). Personality in adulthood: a five-factor theory perspective. New York: Guilford Press.
26. Meddin, J. R. (1998). Dimensions of spiritual meaning and well-being in the lives of ten older Australians. International Journal of Aging and Human Development, 47, 163-175.

27. Midgley, C., Maehr, M. L., Hruda, L. Z., Anderman, E., Anderman, L., Freeman, K. E., ...Urdan, T. (2000). *Manual for the Patterns of Adaptive Learning Scales.* Ann Arbor, MI: University of Michigan Press.
28. Midgley, C., Maehr, M. L., Hruda, L. Z., Anderman, E., Anderman, L., Freeman, K. E., ...Urdan, T. (2000). *Manual for the Patterns of Adaptive Learning Scales.* Ann Arbor, MI: University of Michigan Press.
29. Moffitt, TE, Caspi, A, Rutter, M & Silva, PA (2001). Sex Differences in Antisocial Behavior: Conduct Disorder, Delinquency, and Violence in the Dunedin Longitudinal Study. Cambridge, UK: Cambridge University Press
30. Moller, A. C., & Elliot, A. J. (2006). The 2 × 2 achievement goal framework: An overview of empirical research. In A. V. Mitel (Ed.), *Focus on educational psychology research* (pp. 307–326). New York: Nova Science.
31. Moller, A. C., & Elliot, A. J. (2006). The 2 × 2 achievement goal framework: An overview of empirical research. In A. V. Mitel (Ed.), *Focus on educational psychology research* (pp. 307–326). New York: Nova Science.
32. Murayama, K., Elliot, A. J., & Yamagata, S. (2011). Separation of performance-approach and performance-avoidance achievement goals: A broader analysis. *Journal of Educational Psychology,* 103, 238–256.
33. Murayama, K., Elliot, A. J., & Yamagata, S. (2011). Separation of performance-approach and performance-avoidance achievement goals: A broader analysis. *Journal of Educational Psychology,* 103, 238–256.
34. Nasel, D. D. (2004). Spiritual orientation in relation to spiritual intelligence: A con sideration of traditional Christianity and New Age/individualistic spirituality. Unpublished doctoral dissertation, University of South Australia. Nelson, C., Rosenfeld, B., Breitbart, W., & Galietta, M. (2002) Spirituality, depression and religion in the terminally ill. Psychosomatics, 43, 213-220.
35. Nasel, Dagmar Dasha. (2004). Spiritual orientation in relation to spiritual intelligence: A new consideration of traditional Christianity and New Age/individualistic spirituality. Doctoral Dissertation, Unive-rsity of South Australia: Australia.
36. Nicholls, J. G. (1984). Conceptions of ability and achievement motivation. In R. Ames & C. Ames (Eds.), *Research on motivation in education,* Vol. 1 (pp. 39–73). San Diego, CA: Academic Press.
37. Nicholls, J. G. (1984). Conceptions of ability and achievement motivation. In R. Ames & C. Ames (Eds.), *Research on motivation in education,* Vol. 1 (pp. 39–73). San Diego, CA: Academic Press.

38. Noble, E.P. (2000). The DRD2 gene in psychiatric and neurological disorders and its phenotypes. Pharmacogenomics, 1:309–333.
39. Noble, K. D. (2000). Spiritual intelligence: A new frame of mind. Spirituality and Giftedness, 9, 1-29. Oxford University Press. (2001). Oxford dictionary of current English (3rd ed.). Oxford: Oxford University Press.
40. Oertig, D., Schüler, J., Schnelle, J., Brandstätter, V., Roskes, M., & Elliot, A. J. (2013). Avoidance goal pursuit depletes self-regulatory resources. *Journal of Personality*, 81, 365–375.
41. Oertig, D., Schüler, J., Schnelle, J., Brandstätter, V., Roskes, M., & Elliot, A. J. (2013). Avoidance goal pursuit depletes self-regulatory resources. *Journal of Personality,* 81, 365–375.
42. Park, C. L., &Folkman, S. (1997). Mean ing in the context of stress and coping. Review of General Psychology, 12, 115-144.
43. Pintrich, P. R. (2000). The role of goal orientation in self-regulated learning. In M. Boekarts, P. R. Pintrich, & M. Zeidner (Eds.), *Handbook of self-regulation* (pp. 451–502). San Diego, CA: Academic Press.
44. Pintrich, P. R. (2000). The role of goal orientation in self-regulated learning. In M. Boekarts, P. R. Pintrich, & M. Zeidner (Eds.), *Handbook of self-regulation* (pp. 451–502). San Diego, CA: Academic Press.
45. Reker, G. T. (1997). Personal meaning, optimism, and choice: Existential predicttors of depression in community and institutional elderly. The Gerontologist, 37, 709-716.
46. Reker, G. T., & Wong, P. T. (1988). Aging as an individual process: Toward a theory of personal meaning. In J. E. Birren and V. L. Bengtson (Eds.), Handbook of theories of aging (pp. 214-246). New York: Springer. States, B. (1992). The meaning of dreams. Dreaming. 2, 249-262.
47. Reker, G. T., Peacock, E. J., & Wong, P. T. (1987). Meaning and purpose in life and well-being: A life-span perspective. Journal of Gerontology, 42, 44-49.
48. Ross, M. E., Blackburn, M., & Forbes, S. (2005). Reliability generalization of the Patterns of Adaptive Learning Survey goal orientation Scales. *Educational and Psychological Measurement,* 65, 451–464.
49. Ross, M. E., Blackburn, M., & Forbes, S. (2005). Reliability generalization of the Patterns of Adaptive Learning Survey goal orientation Scales. *Educational and Psychological Measurement,* 65, 451–464.

50. Seybold, K. S., & Hill, P. C. (2001). The role of religion and spirituality in mental and physical health. Current Directions in Psychological Science, 10, 21–24.
51. Shih, S.-S. (2013). Autonomy support versus psychological control, perfectionism, and Taiwanese adolescents' achievement goals. *Journal of Educational Research,* 106, 269–279.
52. Shih, S.-S. (2013). Autonomy support versus psychological control, perfectionism, and Taiwanese adolescents' achievement goals. *Journal of Educational Research,* 106, 269–279.
53. Sinetar, M. (2000). Spiritual intelligence. What we can learn from the early awakening child. Maryknoll, NY: Orbis Books.
54. Sisk, D.A., and Torrance, E. P. (2001). Spiritual Intelligence: Developing Higher Consciousness. Buffalo, NY. Creative Education Foundation.
55. Slade, P. D., & Owens, R. G. (1998). A dual process model of perfectionism based on reinforcement theory. *Behavior Modification,* 22, 372–390.
56. Slade, P. D., & Owens, R. G. (1998). A dual process model of perfectionism based on reinforcement theory. *Behavior Modification,* 22, 372–390.
57. SpeirsNeumeister, K. L., & Finch, H. (2006). Perfectionism in high-ability students: Relational precursors and influences on achievement motivation. *Gifted Child Quarterly,* 50, 238–251.
58. SpeirsNeumeister, K. L., & Finch, H. (2006). Perfectionism in high-ability students: Relational precursors and influences on achievement motivation. *Gifted Child Quarterly,* 50, 238–251.
59. Sternberg, R. J. (1997). The concept of intelligence and its role in lifelong learning and success. American Psychologist, 52, 1030-1037.
60. Stoeber, J. (2011). The dual nature of perfectionism in sports: Relationships with emotion, motivation, and performance. *International Review of Sport and Exercise Psychology*
61. Stoeber, J. (2011). The dual nature of perfectionism in sports: Relationships with emotion, motivation, and performance. *International Review of Sport and Exercise Psychology*
62. Thompson, P. (1992). 'I don't feel old': Subjective ageing and the search for meaning in later life. Ageing and Society, 12, 23-47.
63. Vaughan, F. (2002). What is spiritual intelligence? Journal of Humanistic Psychology, 42, 16-33.
64. Wink, P., & Dillon, M. (2002). Spiritual development across the adult life course: Findings from a longitudinal study. Journal of Adult Development, 9, 79–94.

65. Wolman, R. (2001). Thinking with your soul: Spiritual intelligence and why it matters. Harmony Books, NewYork, 288pp.
66. Wolman, R. N. (2001). Thinking with your soul: Spiritual intelligence and why it matters. New York: Harmony Books.
67. Wong, P. T. (1989). Personal meaning and successful aging. Canadian Psychology, 30, 516-525.
68. Worthington, E. L.,&Sandage, S. J. (2001). Religion and spirituality. Psychotherapy, 38, 473- 478.
69. Zika, S., & Chamberlain, K. (1992). On the relation between meaning in life and psychological well-being. British Jour -nal of Psychology, 83, 133-145.
70. Zohar and Marshall. (2000). SQ: Spiritual intelligence: The ultimate intelligence. London: Bloomsbury.
71. Zohar, D., & Marshall, I. (2000). SQ: Connecting with our spiritual intelligence. New York: Bloomsbury Publishing.
72. Zohar, Danah. (2000). SQ: Connecting with Our Spiritual Intelligence. London: Bloomsbury Vaughan, D. 2002'Media Launch', Contexts Summer: 68–9.
73. Cantor &Kihistrom (1987,1989)
74. O'Sullivan et al. (1965)
75. Riggio. Messamer&Throkmorton, 1991; shanley, walker & Foley, 1971)
76. Burke, Robin(1993)
77. O'Sullivan, M., Guilford, J.P., and Demille, R.(1965)
78. Gupta S (1980) Self Esteem and identification among institutionalized destitute children, page no. V25, N3, P55-67.
79. Hoge Dean R (1990) School experiences predicting changes in Self Esteem.
80. Karunanidhi et al (1996) Problems and gender difference in relation to Self Esteem among adolescents, Journal of Psychological Research nVI & Nv2,P74-80.
81. Mc. Donald et al (1994) Self Esteem in high school students Journal of adolescents V17,N6,P557-564.
82. Pandey (1993) Impact of locus of control on self esteem of college students perspective in Psychological researches VI,P 14-19.
83. Phiney Jean (1992) Accilturation attitude and self esteem among higher secondary school students students, youth and society V23, N3, P299-312.
84. Kubir Singh Sindhu (2009), Methodology of Research in Education, Jalandhar, Sterling publishers LTD.

85. Nagarajan. K (2007), Educational Challenges in the emerging Indian society, Ram Publishers, Chennai.
86. Pattramon Jumpangern (1986); social maturity of higher secondary in Thailand, dissertation abstract international.
87. Puranik, S.D., (1985) A study of the relationship of social maturity of pupils with organizational climate and teachers morale in the primary schools of Bangalore city,Ph.d., Education, Mysore University, Fourth Survey of Research in Education, Buch, M.B., volume 2 (P.111).
88. Sarojamma, Y.H. (1990), Comparative study of teaching ability and social maturity of over, normal and under-achiever of standard VII.
89. Surjit Singh and Dr.PraveenThukrall., (2010) Social maturity and academic achievement of high school students.Candian Journal on scientific and Industrial Research Vol.No.1 July 2010.
90. Beck, J. Gayle; McNiff, Judiann; Clapp, Joshua D.; Olsen, Shira A.; Avery, Carlo, Gustavo; McGinley,Meredith; Davis, Alexandra; Streit, CaraChow, Pizza Ka-Yee; Cheng, Sheung-Tak *Journal of Counseling Psychology*,v57n1 p.92-104 Jan 2010 and Purpose. Islam&Science, 1(1).
91. De Hoyos, Librado R.; Ramirez, Noe *Journal of Ethnic & Cultural Diversity in Social Work,* v15 n1-2 p.147-156 2006 *http://www.tandf.co.uk/journals*
92. Diener, E., Emmons, R.A., Larson, R.J., & Griffin, S. (1985). The satisfaction with life scale. Journal of Personality Assessment, 49, 71-75.
93. Dordrecht, Netherlands: Springer, 2005. Phenomenology of Life: Meating the Challanges of the Present Day World (Analecta Husserliana: The Year Book of Phenomenological Research. Vol. LXXXIV)
94. Efthim, Paul W.; Kenny, Maureen E.; Mahalik, James R. *Journal of Counselling & Development,* v79 n4 p.430-38 Fall 2001
95. Faiver, Christopher M.; O'Brien, Eugene M.; Ingersoll, R. Elliott *Journal of Counselling & Development,* v78 n2 p.155-61 Sep 2000
96. Ferguson, Tamara J.; Stegge, Hedy; Miller, Erin R.; Olsen, Michael E. *Developmental Psychology,* v35 n2 p.347-57 Mar 1999
97. Golshani, Mehdi, 2003. Does Science Offer Evidence of a Transcendent Reality?
98. Grünberg, David, (A) "The Meaning of Life Vis-A-Vis the Challenges of the Present Day World," in Anna-Teresa Tymieniecka (ed.),
99. Grünberg, David, (B) 2005. Etik ve Ya"amın Anlamı, Erdem, 44.
100. Guastello, Stephen, Chaos, Catastrophe, and Human Affairs: Applications of Nonlinear Dynamics to Work, Organizations, and Social Evolution, Lawrence Erlbaum Associates, Mahwah, NJ, 1995.

101. Hesse, Herman, Siddartha, New Directions Paper Book, 1957
102. Hursthouse, Rosalind, 2003, "Virtue Ethics", Stanford Encyclopaedia of Philosophy, Edward N. Zalta (ed.), retrieved 6 April, 2010 from *http://plato.stanford.edu/entries/ethics-virtue/#2*
103. Johnson, Diane Elizabeth *College Student Journal,* v46 n1 p.3-17 Mar 2012
104. Johnson,Veronica R.F.;Yarhouse, Mark A. *Counselling and Values,* v58 n1 p.85-103 Apr 2013
105. Joske, W., D. (2004).Philosophy and the Meaning of Life. In David Benatar (ed.), Life, Death and Meaning: Key Philosophical Readings on the Big Questions (pp.49 – 62). USA, Rowman and Littlefield Publishers Inc. Kraut, Richard, (2001). "Aristotle's Ethics", Stanford Encyclopedia of Philosophy. Retrived August 01, 2010.
106. Kamper, Heidrun *Journal of Multilingual and Multicultural Development,* v25 n5-6 p.497-511 2004
107. Kamper, Heidrun *Journal of Multilingual and Multicultural Development,* v25 n5-6 p.497-511 2004 *http://www.tandf.co.uk/journals*
108. Kim, Jungmeen; Talbot, Nancy L.; Cicchetti, Dante *Child Abuse & Neglect: the International Journal,* v33 n6 p.362-371 Jun 2009
109. Kim, Sangmoon; Thibodeau, Ryan; Jorgensen, Randall S. *Psychological Bulletin,* v137 n1 p.68-96 Jan 2011
110. Kim, Sangmoon; Thibodeau, Ryan; Jorgensen, Randall S. *Psychological Bulletin,* v137 n1 p.68-96 Jan 2011
111. Kolves, Kairi; Ide, Naoko; De Leo, Diego *Suicide and Life-Threatening Behavior,* v41 n2 p.149-159 Apr 2011
112. Konstam, Varda; Chernoff, Miriam; Deveney, Sara *Counselling and Values,* v46 n1 p.26-39 Oct 2001
113. Kristin; Rhea, Deborah J.; Oomen, Jody *American Journal of Health Education,* v35 n3 p.152-157 May-Jun 2004 http://www.aahperd.org
114. Luby, Joan; Belden, Andy; Sullivan, Jill; Hayen, Robin; McCadney, Amber; Spitznagel, Ed *Journal of Child Psychology and Psychiatry,* v50 n9 p.1156-1166 Sep 2009
115. Megan L.; Hagewood, J. Houston *Behavior Therapy,* v42 n4 p.740-750 Dec 2011
116. Meyer, Janet R. *Western Journal of Communication,* v77 n2 p.210-230 2013
117. Mills, R.S.L. *Developmental Review,* v25 n1 p.26-63 Mar 2005
118. *New Directions for Youth Development,* n136 p.75-93 Win 2012

119. Thomaes, Sander; Stegge, Hedy; Olthof, Tjeert *British Journal of Developmental Psychology,* v25 n4 p.559-577 Nov 2007
120. Updike, Thomas L., Jr.; And Others Psychology: *A Quarterly Journal of Human Behavior,* v24 n1-2 p.60-64 1987
121. Wietzker, Anne; Buysse, Ann *Psychological Assessment,* v24 n3 p.783-789 Sep 2012
122. Wiginton, Kristin; Rhea, Deborah J.; Oomen, Jody *American Journal of Health Education,* v35 n3 p.152-157 May-Jun 2004
123. Wiginton, Kristin; Rhea, Deborah J.; Oomen, Jody *American Journal of Health Education,* v35 n3 p.152-157 May-Jun 2004
124. Williams, Kate; Donaghue, Ngaire; Kurz, *Tim Psychology of Women Quarterly,* v37 n1 p.97-112 Mar 2013
125. Williams, Neil F. *Journal of Physical Education, Recreation & Dance,* v86 n1 p.36-39 2015
126. Wilson, Tom *Journal of Education & Christian Belief,* v18 n2 p.155-169 2014

❑❑❑